Hickory Road

Stories from Hickory Hollow

Roy L. French

PublishAmerica
Baltimore

© 2011 by Roy L. French
All rights reserved. No part of this book may be reproduced, stored in a retrieval system or transmitted in any form or by any means without the prior written permission of the publishers, except by a reviewer who may quote brief passages in a review to be printed in a newspaper, magazine or journal.

First printing

PublishAmerica has allowed this work to remain exactly as the author intended, verbatim, without editorial input.

Hardcover 978-1-4560-3824-3
Softcover 978-1-4560-3825-0
PUBLISHED BY PUBLISHAMERICA, LLLP
www.publishamerica.com
Baltimore

Printed in the United States of America

Acknowledgments

Thanks go to the people who touched my life and contributed to this undertaking in subtle ways. Most may not have realized their influences. To all, I say thank you. This book could not have come about without the dedication and hard work of my good friend, Mickey Olson, who believed this project was worth the effort. Without her encouragement and typing skills, the book may not have come to fruition.

I especially appreciate my father, Dave, and mother, Marie French, for all the hardships they endured in raising us three boys and twin girls on a carpenter's wages. Dave was a good provider and Marie kept the home fires burning and fed us well.

As a quiet child who stuttered some, I remember the best times as those when aunts and uncles came to visit and filled our small home in the hollow. The men would gather in the front room while the women sat in the kitchen. I would sit in the doorway between the two rooms so I could hear the stories coming from both rooms as they told and retold their adventures of growing up and the fun they had. Later on, as bedtime came, I would drift off to sleep with Dad and Mom, and Dad's brothers and sisters still talking about good times past. I remember feeling that all was right in the world and the house in the hollow was the best place to be.

The stories they told stayed with me until in later years I wrote them down. Some of them are in this book.

Table of Contents

The Big City Cure 7
Our Winter World 14
Christmas Boots 16
The Trap Line 19
A Winter Hound 24
Blue Flannel Lining 30
Cooking on the Old Heatrola 34
Ungiven Gift 37
Pink Valentine, Red Face 40
Potato Harvest 45
Fall of Forty-One 48
A Blessing of Ducks 67
The War Years 71
Firecrackers 74
Grand Essentials 77
Never Can Go Back They Say 82
Eyeglasses 85
Of a Certain Persuasion 88
Where Angels Play 92
The Last Christmas Cards 98
The Drifting Ball Pitcher 103

Thatcher's Barn	107
The Radio	112
Season of Hope	115
Winter Doldrums and Lion Dogs	118
Angel Maudie	121
The Heart Remembers	125
Fine Folk and Shivarees	128
Winter Comforts	131
Ice Storms and Kids	134
For as Long as We Can	137
The Chandler Place	139
New Salem Christmas	145
Gwyn's Skating	150
Gooseberries	153
March of March	156
The Silence of the Wood	159
About The Author	162

The Big City Cure

Unable to adjust to or enjoy living in town, Dave's father, Will, had made a decision to return to the woods. His preference for hard work and the calling of the hills along the Sangamon Valley were greater for him than the comforts of city life. At the same time, he had lost all his life savings in the closing of a local bank. Now, at 66 years of age, Will yearned for a measure of peace within himself to live out his years.

Dave's mother, Dena, remained at their home on Job Street at the west end of town. Dave worked in the country with his dad while living with his mother in town. His sisters had married and moved north. One lived in Peoria. Two brothers married and moved to Alton to find work and a better way of life. It was clear to Dave that his family would never again be as it was before.

With a separated home life, Marie had come down from Wisconsin for the summer to visit her father, who was a construction worker, fisherman, and farmer as well as a part-time tent preacher near Beardstown. She chanced to come with neighbors to a dance in the upstairs Trotter's Hall in Virginia. There she met Dave. He was a well dressed dandy of twenty-six with wavy hair, and she a bright and trim girl of eighteen with a crisp Wisconsin way of talking.

The dance was good, the music sweet, the signs were right, and romance was romance. She looked deep inside of him while he looked deep inside her. They each saw a strength in the other that would add to their own. Seeing once close family bonds coming apart created in them a great and urgent need to form a bond themselves and fill an emptiness they were both feeling.

Dave and Marie were married by the justice of the peace in April of 1929. Neither was able to bring much in the way of material goods to the union nor were their folks in a position to offer anything in the way of resources, either household or monetary. So Dave and Marie set off to form and build their own secure and comfortable world just a few months before the stock market crash of 1929.

Marie had all she owned in a suitcase. Dave had a few hounds and a Model T pickup. Even though it was more than ten years old, it was a trusty truck, good for both work and travel.

They were happy through the summer, full of energy and good times on a shoestring. They added to their security but Dave realized he'd need a better job if he were going to provide for a wife and future family. By fall Marie was pregnant, and settling down to a good job was serious business for Dave.

As winter came, Dave was more restless and determined to make good, and he was missing his sister, Gladys. Gladys had a snug and secure home in Peoria just off Monroe Street, not far from the river and Caterpillar Tractor Manufacturing Plant. She had been close to her brothers, and they all returned to her for that old familiar comfort and closeness of days gone by.

A few days before Christmas, Dave watched the snow come down from the front window of his mother's house in Virginia. "Marie," he said, "I'd like to go to Gladys as soon as the snow lets up. Maybe we can go up that way in the morning." There was Dave next to his mother, missing his sister, loving his wife who was with child, and it was Christmas.

Dave slept restlessly that night in the hushed silence of the snow. He thought of looking for work in Peoria, of getting an apartment of their own with running water, and a better existence for his wife and child. As the room brightened with the first morning light, he kissed his sleeping wife, then got up and scraped the frost from the window to look out. He whispered, "Marie Honey, the snow has stopped."

Before long they were in the Model T going to Peoria. The side curtains had been made tight. They wrapped themselves in blankets and put a kerosene lantern on the floor between them for heat. Coffee was in a thermos, and lunch was in a sack.

It was a long, arduous trip over snow-packed and icy roads by way of Ashland and Tallula, with a broken wheel at Petersburg, over the Sangamon, and on east. As the miles passed one by one, Dave's chest filled with a feeling of excitement. Soon they connected with the new superhighway Route 29 and turned north to Mason City where they bought gas and oil, and ate sandwiches before heading toward Green Valley and Pekin. Icicles were hanging from the radiator and axles. Snow had packed under the fenders and running boards as Dave drove over the river bridge into Peoria.

He relaxed and loosened his grip on the wheel. They had come a long, long way under difficult conditions. Sister Gladys' warm house on LaVielle Street was calling him just as sure as a star guided others a long time ago. The early winter darkness was coming on as they drove along Monroe Street, dodging street cars and people on foot as they looked through the frosty windshield for LaVielle Street and Gladys' house. Then there it was—610 LaVielle Street. A light was in the window.

The homecoming was a joyous occasion. Dave was glad to have his wife in a warm and comfortable place on the night before Christmas. He felt happiness and contentment in being with his sister again. Not often did they let emotions show, but they were expressed freely with hugs and kisses on rosy cheeks by those gathered in that small house.

Gladys made fresh, perked coffee on the gas stove and sliced ham for sandwiches. They ate and visited about old times and good times far into the night.

Later, when Dave and Marie lay holding each other warm and deep under soft old quilts in the east bedroom, all the world was right again. He said to her in a low voice, "Don't lessen this Christmas with worry about gifts. We can't afford any. But the feeling pulsing inside me now and the life pulsing inside you are the greatest gifts either of us could ever hope for. Any other gifts would just lessen this Christmas." They drifted off into a deep and wondrous sleep in the silent winter night.

***

Dave especially enjoyed the hounds and roaming the hills and valleys where he grew up. He felt an intimacy with all outdoors and knew of many sylvan settings with Clearwater streams and flowering meadows. But in search of a better life, Dave decided it was best to leave the outdoor life and find more stable work and wages. In the weeks that followed their arrival in Peoria, Dave applied for work at Caterpillar Tractor and was soon called in to work the early shift.

It was not long before he and his wife found a three-room apartment over a grocery store on Northeast Adams Street. A bedroom window to the east allowed Dave to see the river and the wooded hills on the other side. "This would do," he thought.

The weeks passed quickly. They were adjusting to city life. Within a few months Dave's foreman called him to one side and said, "Davey, how'd you like to be a welder? I believe you could learn it fast." Dave agreed, knowing that it cost a lot to live in Peoria and welders made good wages. Soon Dave was spot welding the sheet metal that went on large combines destined for the wheat fields of Russia.

The summer came and went. Dave and his wife were doing as well as any young couple just starting out. Fall was upon them and the leaves were turning. About the time he heard the first migrating geese overhead, there were newspaper headlines about trouble in the stock market. By Thanksgiving, it began to affect the industries. Over turkey and dressing at his sister's, they discussed what it might be like by Christmas.

Dave came out of the plant on a Friday afternoon in a contemplative mood. It was early December but the air was soft as if the earth had breathed. "Wild game will run tonight," he thought. He leaned against his Model T truck and felt the gentle warmth of the low December sun. He ate a candy bar while gazing across the river.

His day dreaming was interrupted by a stray hound trotting across the lot. Dave focused on him and called. The dog stopped, perked up his ears, and looked right at Dave. He had a good looking head and shiny coat. "Here, Boy!" Dave called and pitched a piece of candy bar in the dog's direction. The dog ate it and came a bit closer. Dave tossed another morsel till the dog was within arm's reach. He leaned to pet him, touching a dog for the first time in months. The dog was friendly with wagging tail and happy eyes. Dave reached into his truck for twine, knotted it around the dog's neck, and in a minute had it sitting beside him in the seat. Dave was elated. He had a dog, never mind how he'd gotten it. Off they went in Dave's Model T over the lift bridge toward Adams Street, like old friends and old times.

There was time left in the late afternoon and Dave had a plan. Coon hunting was something he thoroughly enjoyed. Now he had the chance. He would take his new dog to Spring Bay and hunt with friends there.

Dave made a hurried explanation to his wife, who was very perplexed at him having a dog. In the small apartment, he mixed some bread crust and left over corn bread with milk to feed to the dog that ate his fill with wagging tail. After a quick supper himself, Dave kissed his wife, and then with his dog under his arm, he was off. It was dark when he arrived at the upriver village. There was much to say about Dave's new dog. What a fine looking hound he was and shouldn't they try him out. "What's the dog's name?" someone asked. Dave hadn't thought about a name, but thinking quickly, he remembered the candy bar and confidently said, "The dog's name is Hershey." His friends were amused, but Dave was serious and said, "Let's get the lanterns and run us some coon."

Hershey pulled hard on the leash and sniffed the air of the river bottom. They were some distance out toward a backwater slough. Dave unsnapped the dog. "Go get 'em, Boy," he coaxed. Just at the edge of their lantern light, a cottontail bounded from a thicket and passed right in front of Hershey. The dog took off like a bullet, running the rabbit by sight, barking every breath through the woods and willow breaks for maybe a quarter of a mile or so. The barking faded. Dave was embarrassed. A good coon dog never chases rabbits, and his friends had a great time laughing and kidding him about it. Dave called and called. They listened. They waited. But the dog did not return. It was clear that Hershey wouldn't hunt.

Dave returned to the small apartment with the window on the river. His wife lay sleeping under old quilts that moved with her quiet breathing. He looked out to see Christmas lights shining on the far bluff and saw their reflections in the rippling water. Dave felt melancholy, and the wetness in his own eyes multiplied the colors and reminded him of windows in the Sangamon Valley Church. There would be singing there on Christmas Eve, and the echoing peal of the church bell. The thought made him feel so far from home.

He lay awake listening to the sounds of the city and thought of the intensity of life going on around him, of people hurrying, each one faster than the other, with no time to touch their own feelings, absent from all things natural, removed from peace, solitude erased. It was not his kind of Christmas.

Dave, in the closure of his eyes, could see winter landscapes of white frost sparkling in silent moonlight on Ainsworth Hill, the hushed tracery of snow on twigs and branches along the wagon road up Warner's hollow, the clear, spring-fed streams along Schaad Creek. He heard the owl, the jay, and the bay of a hunting hound in a land where he breathed in what the earth breathed out, and all God's gifts were close at hand. Visions of the valley ebbed and flowed throughout the night.

Dave opened his eyes to a room becoming light and saw the pinkening sky of a rising winter sun and a river all aglow. It was as a promise to him liken to a rainbow, a promise that he would never spend another Christmas away from comforting folds of the Sangamon Valley.

Our Winter World

By this time last year we had been snowed in here on Indian Run Creek, and each time it happened, I thought of our home in the 1930's and 40's over in Hickory Hollow a few miles from where I live now. I imagine we were snowed in there many times but didn't know it. The biggest snow I remember as a boy came in November and was so deep that a little fox terrier dog we had made jumps in the snow like a rabbit to keep going. Each time he'd stop, his belly would rest in the snow with his feet not touching the ground. Of course, the cold on his underside just made him jump again.

Dad made a small "V" plow out of some oak boards, put a heavy stone on it, and pulled it around to make paths to the barn, the wash house, the root cellar, the well, and of course, the outhouse which was just past the wood pile. These were the only paths necessary for us to travel.

As most families of that era, we could have lived a great length of time traveling those paths and using those things the earth in Hickory Hollow had given us, and Mom, Dad, and Grandpa had stored away. The four acres of that hollow fed us five kids, Mom, Dad, and Grandpa and most anyone else who came to visit. Grandpa did a lot of gardening and was an important member of the family.

We had a rather common Jersey cow, and hay was put up loose in the barn for her to exchange for milk, cream, butter, cottage cheese, and usually a bull calf every year, much to Dad's disgust. He would have preferred a heifer.

Carpenter work and sawmill work was about over the first of December, but by then Dad had the trap line out for many miles around, and the coon hounds were ready to go each night. So cash was coming in a little at a time and there always seemed to be enough. I never felt we were poor and now that I've grown older, I know for sure we weren't in the many ways that people are poorer now.

We had a few hens but if they were off their laying, we walked through the timber and pasture to Frank Warner's and bought a dozen for twelve to thirteen cents, depending on what the market was. Mr. Warner always had a little kerosene for our lamps if we needed it, too. His place was a fifteen minute walk southeast. Aunt Daisy and Uncle George lived a half hour up the west hollow and were always glad to see us. Hickory Church and School were about a mile or twenty minutes north over the famous hill. And that was about as big as our winter world was or needed to be. There were family and friends, water, fuel, meat, school, church, and entertainment closer in travel time then than today. Only at that time, we didn't depend on foreign oil, generating plants, or fancy roads. A different kind of person lives in the country today and depends on many outside sources. I guess that is progress and shouldn't be tampered with.

Christmas Boots

I remember many Christmas times past, but one in particular returned to me the other day as I went looking for some new overshoes for winter. There on a shelf in the shoe store was a pair of knee high rubber boots, the kind I wanted so many years ago.

In the late thirties I was just a little shaver but still I had been on the trap line with Dad, and at each stream or creek he had to carry me across. My little overshoes were just not tall enough to wade through the water and mud. We lived on Schaad Creek and all of us kids found the creek to be an endless and ever-changing playground. With each big rain, the water changed course a little and made new pools and gravel beds to study. Occasionally we found an arrowhead or spear point. So much wildlife used the creek for traveling from the Sangamon bottoms to the prairie and, of course, left a record of their passing by making footprints in the mud and snow of Schaad Creek. We watched minnows under the ice in winter and tadpoles and pollywogs in summer. There was always something to do in the creek. But many times we misjudged the strength and thickness of the ice and got a foot wet. At other times, what looked like solid ground turned into watery mud a little more than shoe top high, and again we'd go to the house with a cold and wet, muddy foot to dry off by the Heatrola.

That year, as the chill of December deepened and Christmas neared, I wished for a pair of knee high rubber boots. With knee boots, I wouldn't have to worry about deep snow or getting my feet wet as I walked in the creek or on the trap line.

In our family that had reached three kids by then Christmas was a close time. There were the church programs over at Hickory and school activities that kept our little minds and imaginations busy. We knew better than to ask for lots of gifts. We had to narrow things down to what we wanted most and, of course, it had to be practical, something that was needed and useful. I thought knee boots were just the thing for a boy like me. So each time I got a chance, I'd mention how fine some boots would be. I stayed on my best behavior and watched the days and waited.

Dad brought home a Cedar tree, the only kind of Christmas tree we knew, and he put it in the corner of the front room by the Crosley radio. We decorated it with the one strand of angel hair that we kept from year to year, paper chains, strings of popcorn, and Mom's Wisconsin cranberries.

The winter so far had been a good one. The fur from Dad's trap line kept coming in. The wood pile was still ricked high, and the root cellar stored plenty of the necessary things. Dad kept fresh game hanging in the smokehouse ready to add a little variety to our meals. Still, money was scarce at this time of year, especially for buying Christmas gifts.

Finally Christmas Eve came. My older brother Jack, younger brother Billy, and I went to bed as excited as ever, each wishing for some special present. We were restless and turned and tossed. But in awhile I heard my brothers' measured breathing as they dropped off to sleep. I soon followed.

Sometime later in the night, I woke up. I didn't know how much time had passed. I could still hear my brothers sleeping.

The kerosene lamp turned low on the front room table filled the night as candlelight. The fire had died away in the heating stove. The house was cold and still, and it was Christmas. Had Santa been there? Was it near morning? I had feelings of excitement and mystery. Slowly I rolled back the covers, moved as silently as I could, and peeked around the corner of the doorway. There, not two feet from my nose, was not one but three pairs of shiny new rubber boots. What a beautiful sight. A big pair of boots for brother Jack, a smaller pair for brother Billy John, and another pair just right for me. My prayers had been answered. My boots were right there.... Or was I in a dream? I reached out and touched them. They were real! I looked inside and saw that someone had written my name in them. They were mine. Quietly I picked them up and slipped my feet into them. They felt so-o-o-o good and I felt very tall. I was the happiest kid in the world.

    I stood there beside the Christmas tree in my baggy long johns and brand new boots, not knowing what to do. Should I take them off and go back to bed? Could I go to bed with them on? Goodness no. If I put them back under the tree, would they still be there in the morning? I didn't want to take them off. I wouldn't give them up. So I curled up on the end of the davenport closest to the Christmas tree and drifted back to sleep, still wearing my brand new knee high rubber boots. And that's where Dad and Mom found me and my boots on Christmas morning.

The Trap Line

I would not be six till early May and it was only January. I had wanted a pair of knee-high rubber boots, the shiny kind I had seen in the catalog, and I did get a pair for Christmas. I was proud of my new rubber boots and wore them all Christmas Day.

But now it was past Christmas and into a new year. My older brother Jack was back at Hickory School in the third grade. My little brother was only two. I didn't have much to do.

The weather had moderated some. Dad had about finished his chores of milking the Jersey cow, feeding the old sow, gathering the eggs and feeding his hounds.

Hunting season was over for him. Trapping season was over too. I think he had ten days from the first of January to get his traps collected and to get rid of the fur. The weather had been so bad he couldn't get to his trap line, but now with the weather moderating a little, he was anxious to go get his traps and have them ready for next season. It was a job he had to do. There wasn't much pleasure in it for him.

It had been a good trapping season and Dad was a good trapper. He was called "Trapper Dave" by his friends and hunting buddies. He caught several mink, muskrats, dozens of raccoons, many red foxes and a number of possums and skunks, much to his disgust. A person was allowed twenty-five traps per license. Dad had a trapping license, Mom had a trapping license, Grandpa had a trapping license and my older brother Jack, at age eight, had a trapping license. That made a hundred traps Dad could set out. He had three trap lines he would run every other day during trapping season. George, a fur buyer from Virginia, would come every couple of weeks. They would climb in the barn loft where Dad hung his fur, and haggle over the price till all was satisfied. It was commonplace to see a check of eighty or one hundred dollars for fur. That was a lot of money in those days, but it had to last till spring when carpenter work would open up again.

But now it was time for him to take up the traps. Mom said, "Why don't you take Roy Lee with you? It's warming up some. The sun is out. Get him out of the house for a change." Even though I didn't care much for trapping, I was all for it. Dad didn't much like the idea. I was born with some foot problems and might slow him down. He thought about that and said he'd take me on one of the shorter trap lines.

I said, "Can I wear my new rubber boots?"

Dad said, "Why don't you wear the shoes you got on? Put your overshoes on. They'll be fine."

"No, I want to wear my new rubber boots. Can't I?" I pleaded. "Well, okay. Go get them on," he said.

I was a kid enthused. I put on a good pair of socks and slid my feet into the new boots. They felt good. I put on my coat, sock cap, and gloves. I was ready to do what big men do — gather the traps.

We went out by the smokehouse, walked by the garden fence, up past the barn and on to the gate that led to the pasture. Once through the gate, we were on our way to the trap line. We cut up a timbered ridge on a well-worn path for about a mile to where Warner's fence line ran. We crossed some prairie and came to a deep, wide hollow where Dad had a lot of traps set.

HICKORY ROAD

Dad was a strong walker. He got so far ahead of me that I had to run to catch up. It was tiring. I fell a lot but was quick to get up again and continue on. My boots were not gripping the ground like I thought they would. My right boot was eating my sock and was uncomfortable, but I walked on, not wanting to slow my dad or become a nuisance.

I was glad when Dad stopped under a tree. He said it was an Apple tree. With his foot, he felt around in the deep grasses, and pretty soon he came upon a lump. It was an apple. He gave it to me and said, "Eat it. You'll like it." It was a bit sour but cold and tasted good. He found another and we spent a few minutes eating apples. It would be the best part of the day.

He had a mink and a muskrat in his traps. Some traps were thrown with nothing in them. He took up a dozen sets in the stream that made its way through Pete Tyford's pasture. He took up two fox sets up on the flats and continued on. I sat on the edge of a cow path by the creek and hurriedly pulled off my boot and straightened my sock.

We crossed behind the Reid place and headed west and crossed Hickory Road, and then we made our way over to Charlie Barr's land where Dad had more traps. He had a coon and some possum toes in those sets. He was loaded down with two dozen traps, a mink, muskrat, and now a coon. Even with his load, he was walking far out ahead of me. My right boot was eating my sock again, and I thought I was getting a blister on my heel. Why didn't I wear my high top shoes and overshoes like Dad had wanted me to? I began to hate my shiny boots I had gotten for Christmas.

I thought we'd be home by noon, but we weren't. I was cold. I was hungry, and I was tired. And we weren't near home yet.

I began lagging behind Dad quite a ways. We came to an old logging road cut through the timber. We followed it through the trees. Dad was getting farther and farther ahead, but if I followed the old logging road, I wouldn't lose sight of him. We came to a place where the logging road went down the hill. I lost sight of Dad and I was frightened. I ran ahead and caught sight of him at the bottom of the hill. He was crossing the creek where a log bridge had once been. With the traps and furs, he made a run between the logs and rustled up the other side.

When I got to the creek, there was a layer of slippery mud on top of the frozen ground, thawed by the afternoon sun. I tried to cross and climb up the other bank, but it was too slippery and I fell in the mud. I was exhausted. I began to cry. I sobbed and sobbed while I lay in the mud and water in the creek bottom. I thought Dad had gone off and left me. I felt abandoned and all by myself.

It seemed like a long time passed. Dad walked another fifty yards to Hickory Road, unloaded his traps and fur to get a little rest. It was then that he came back to get me. "What's the matter, boy? Can't you cross a little creek?" he said. "Come on, give me your hand. I'll pull you up."

I stopped crying and reached up for Dad's hand. He pulled me up. I was muddy and wet and glad to be on solid ground. I followed Dad back to Hickory Road. He picked up his fur and traps. By now, we were only about a half mile from the house, and I knew that part of the road pretty well. We trudged on home.

Something changed in me that day. I didn't care about trapping any more. I didn't care for my shiny boots, and most of all, with my club feet, I found out that I couldn't keep up. I realized I was not a favorite son and never would be.

Darkness settled in early that afternoon and the kerosene lamp didn't do much to brighten the room. At suppertime Dad recalled the events of the day, of finding the apples and getting the mink. I didn't have much to say to anybody. My feelings were still hurt. When it was bedtime, I thought about what I had gone through during the day. I had a lump in my throat and held back tears as I fell asleep that night.

The next day I stayed close to Mom, following her around the house, spending time by the Heatrola heating stove. I was still trying to figure things out. Where was my place in the family? I remember playing by myself a lot. I played in Schaad Creek watching minnows, saw how ice formed over pools, found some pretty rocks, saw game tracks along the shores, and followed rabbit tracks in the snow. I was a contented child, but from that time on, I would become closer to my mother. She called me Roy Boy. I liked that.

We had creek to cross on the trapline.

A Winter Hound

This past Thanksgiving, during a time away and a walk in the woods, I heard the clear, far-off call of a hound. It must have come from a mile or so away. It was a fine voice, full and deep, carried along on the still evening air.

I heard it again coming from somewhere out of my childhood. It stirred in my remembrances of seventy years ago, when hounds were part of our life and family.

Dave, my dad, had his Baldy dog, a strong black and tan hound so smart that my dad and the dog knew each other's thoughts. It was a bonding companionship like no other.

Glenn, a neighbor down on the Sangamon bottom, had Belle, a small, yet older dog with a good nose that could follow the coldest trail. Glenn and Dave ran their dogs together when time and weather permitted—chased foxes by day and raccoons by night.

Having a good reliable hunting dog in the winter season was almost an economic necessity for rural folks, especially during the lean years before the war. The pelt of a raccoon was equal to two days' wages and a prime fox fur was near equal to a whole week's work in dollars and cents. When Dave's carpenter work tailed off toward winter, the hunting skills of man and dog supplemented the family income.

On a December morning, under a clear sky and a full sun, Dave and Glenn walked their hounds east up the bottom road to the Taylor ground, then south along the banks of Indian Run Creek. Where the lowland met the hills, they turned the dogs loose to run.

Foxes often left their dens to lie in the sun on such a day and it wasn't long till the barking hounds told of a chase.

The men were invigorated, their spirits high. They shared a mutual pleasure in being outdoors, breathing in the fresh air, the subtle fragrances of woodland and stream and panoramas of winter landscapes along the valley.

Dave and Glenn stopped to listen as Baldy and Belle echoed down Warner's Hollow, then came into full view some quarter mile away. The quick fox ran some distance ahead, resplendent in red coat and full plume of tail.

The joy of the hunt was on. The men followed the hounds on south and saw them crest hills and ridges, each time a little more in the distance. By mid-afternoon, they could no longer hear the dogs.

Baldy and Belle would have been tired. The fox had played his tricks and more than likely returned to his den. The men called their dogs in. Only Baldy came. They called again and waited, but Belle did not show. Surely she would come later. It was time to go.

Dave snapped a chain on his dog and began to lead him away. Baldy was reluctant to go, kept pulling back. Dave lost patience, admonished his dog to forget the fox, and led him off toward the bottom road.

The wind had changed. A heavy northwest sky covered the sun and its warmth. Overhead, ducks and geese were returning from the fields to the protection of backwater sloughs and open water along the Sangamon. The men felt the weather would be much different by morning and voiced concern over Belle not coming in. When they reached Hickory Road by the church and school they parted, each going his own way toward home.

Dave, in his trek over the hill with his hound, watched and listened for Belle. Between the gusts of wind, he imagined at times he could hear a barking cry, but he continued on.

Dave was greeted by his wife, Marie, and his children as he came into the little house by the creek and found it comfortably warm. The aroma of supper heating on the cook stove, the decorated tree in the corner by the radio, a well and happy family gave him much to be thankful for that season. Yet the gnawing worry of Belle still out there dampened his feelings.

As they ate supper by lamplight, he recounted the day's hunt to Marie and the children about the fox and then the absence of Belle. He became lost in thought, reviewing all the dangers for a hunting dog—the horned cattle, occasional wolves, gates, fences and animal traps.

Just a few days before on his own trap line, Dave had visited with Mr. Ross as he repaired his line fence by adding a new strand of barbed wire above the others, the kind with double barbs. Dave recalled them looking especially vicious. The thought startled him and came forward in his mind. Would the new wire, just a bit higher, keep an older dog from jumping clear? If Belle's leg caught on those barbs, she would be there yet. A hunter's worst nightmare is having his dog hung in a fence.

Dave stepped out the back door and struck a match to see the thermometer. Seventeen degrees it read. "A dog would not last long in that," he thought. Dave could not contain himself. Back in the house he said, "Marie, I've got to go see if I can find that dog. I think I know where she might be."

Marie cautioned him, "It's pretty late to be going out. What if it starts to snow like the radio says?"

It was to no avail. "I'll be all right. Baldy will be with me," he replied.

"Do you have your compass?" she quizzed.

"No," Dave said. "I never need a compass in the hills." With that he gathered on all his winter clothes—the hunting coat, overshoes, double gloves and a heavy cap. He put his big flashlight in the game pocket of his coat, filled the lantern with kerosene, and snapped a chain on Baldy. They set out, both anxious as could be to search for Belle.

Just past the barn lot, a cow path led southeast, a familiar route common to Dave's feet and an avenue to many hunts. It climbed a gentle timbered ridge. They were a hundred yards along with Baldy pulling hard on the chain when Dave felt the first bits of sleet strike his face and rattle the leaves around them.

"Snow will follow," he thought. They hurried on and came out of the woods at Warner's pasture, a wide expanse of prairie before them. It would be a long walk to Ross's line fence. The sleet had changed to snow and was coming down at a good rate. Baldy pulled a steady course.

Dave shined the light ahead, then right and left, again and again, but the snow limited the visual distance to only a few yards. They moved cautiously for a long time in the disorienting night.

Baldy was the first to find the fence. He stopped abruptly, sniffed the air, and turned south. Dave shined the light ahead as they moved from post to post. Somewhere up ahead he caught a reflection. A tag or an eye. Then it disappeared. There it was again. Dave and Baldy ran to it, and there was old Belle with a hind leg snagged in the wire, head hanging down, forepaws just touching the ground. Belle was stiff and cold.

Dave lifted her gently and saw the gash and the exposed tendons where the barbs had caught. He untangled the leg from the wires and heard the dog whimper. Belle was alive.

He lowered her to the ground but she could not stand. Dave sat down, gathered her up as he would one of his children, opened his coat and cradled her next to his warmth. He took snow, melted it in his hand, and held it to Belle's nose. She licked at it. Again and again, she licked the melted snow and swallowed. Her stiffness relaxed. She began to warm.

Dave knew they could not stay. There was a long way to go and the snow had obliterated their tracks. There were no sounds or sights to orient him. On leaving the fence, he could soon lose his way. Dave wished he had listened to his wife and put the compass in his pocket. He would have to depend on his dog to find the way.

With an arm across his coat holding Belle inside, the other hand holding the lantern and a chain, they struck out into the featureless white with Baldy out front.

It seemed they walked miles. Dave wondered if maybe they were lost and going in circles, but he trusted his dog. They rested then moved on again into the deepening snow.

Dave stepped into a shallow place and nearly lost his footing but recognized at once the familiar contours of the cow path that would lead them home. He felt relief. His face flushed with joy and an enormous love for his winter hound. Baldy had guided them through the trackless snow to just the right place.

They were only yards from the house before they saw the golden glow of lamplight through the swirling snow. Dave called out loudly, then called again. As Marie opened the door, all creatures entered in—snow covered, cold and exhausted.

Dave fell to his knees in front of the cook stove. Belle slid out of his coat into the surrounding warmth and soon was covered with blankets. They were all safely home, and Belle was going to be all right.

At such a time emotions well up and become evident even in strong men. They did in Dave as he petted the two hounds there by the stove.

Dave and Marie nursed Glenn's dog for several days, cleaning the wound and covering it with carbolic salve. Belle drank and she ate and soon was able to stand.

The roads were drifted with snow so deep that Dave, Marie, the children, and the dogs were isolated there in the hollow till just days before Christmas. It was then that Belle was strong enough to travel, although with a graceful limp.

Dave and Baldy walked her north to Glenn's house down on the bottom, giving over to him the finest Christmas present he would receive—old Belle, his winter hound.

Blue Flannel Lining

We were luckier than most. Mom and Dad developed many survival skills between them. They shared areas of interest and possessed a perpetual drive to earn, provide, and support through very difficult circumstances and very lean times.

When carpenter work played out in late fall, Dad began his hunting to keep fresh meat on our table. His skills and miles of trap lines rewarded us with fur to sell and a steady winter income.

The activities of providing for a large family created the exercise that kept us all healthy, and we children could see the effort and sacrifice and never begged for more than we had.

It was a December day, short on daylight through a hazy sky. I had been down along the creek for much of the morning discovering animal tracks and watching the play of cold, clear water making its way over rocks and sand, then disappearing under thin lacy edges of white ice before silently stealing away to larger pools of clear ice that became windows for seeing minnows swimming beneath. It provided me a great pleasure with discoveries end on end.

But I had seen enough. Though the sun was not out, I knew it was near noon and I was cold. Mother had not yet made my winter coat. Other children came first and I would get mine in proper order.

When I walked through the back door into the kitchen, I met the satisfying aroma of rich potato soup simmering on the cook stove. We had grown the potatoes and onions, and milk came from our Jersey cow. A rich halo of butter ringed the pot. It was delicious by itself, but we always extended it with saltine crackers. Life was good, my tummy would soon be full.

Mom said to me, "Roy Lee, come into the front room a minute." There, scattered on the chair and couch, were lots of unfamiliar clothing. A family from down on the bottom road had dropped off a big box of hand-me-downs their children had outgrown. Mother had gone through it with great delight considering it all a gift, an answer to her silent prayers.

Mother asked me to stand still while she held different articles of clothing up to me. I felt the textures, noticed the colors, the designs and fancy buttons. She held up a large gray coat with holes in the elbows. She said it was wool and would keep me warm. There was a soft blue shirt, a flannel one, she said. It felt good to my hands, felt good against my face. The gray and blue looked good, one with the other. She put them to one side by the rocker. All the other garments went back into the box for another time.

Mother began working on the coat almost at once. With a razor blade, she began loosening the seams to lay out odd shaped pieces on the front room floor. She made patterns for my size from saved grocery sacks. For smaller pieces, she used newspaper. She pinned the pattern to the gray wool, avoiding the elbow holes, then trimmed around the paper. I saw how a sleeve was made, how the collar was to lay.

In the days that followed and as time permitted, she sewed on the coat. I saw it progress. She sat at her Singer sewing machine for long periods, her feet running the treadle that turned a wheel that ran a belt that powered the needle.

On good days, when the constant edge of stress and worry had backed away to a comfortable distance, Mother sewed at her Singer with great joy and skill. As she treadled, she whistled, and the sound of the two gave me a good feeling that all in the hollow was in harmony, and God lived nearby with a watchful eye.

It was the last day of school before Christmas vacation. As I came home from Hickory School, the winter sun was already low in the sky. I came into the warmth of the front room. Mom said, "Roy Lee, I finished your coat this afternoon. Want to try it on?"

I put my hand to the inside and felt the flannel lining. I smiled up at Mother. She said, "You can wear it outside to play, but be careful with it."

The sun was strong enough yet that I was drawn towards it. I crossed the creek, went up the west hollow and took a slow angling cow path up the south side of a hill in Uncle Troy's pasture. I climbed high and looked down on a beautiful sylvan setting. The jay called. The crow answered. The coat was warm. I lay down on deep tufts of wintering bluegrass. It was immensely quiet. I opened my coat and felt the blue flannel lining. I folded it toward my face to feel the same warmth and comfort, to see my mother's stitching, to see fabric where only paper patterns had been a few days before. I felt an internal happiness and warmth like no other. No Christmas present would be better than my new coat Mother had made for me.

I have carried that memory with me for seventy years or so. I returned to that hillside a few days ago as I often do this time of year. The jay still calls, the crow still answers. I sat down on the deep soft tufts of wintering bluegrass and recalled the softness of that blue flannel lining. I know you can better explain silk after you have felt sackcloth, better appreciate your mother's sewing after you have gone without, after her hands no longer sew. I have had some very fine Christmases.

Cooking on the Old Heatrola

With what people called the energy problem we experienced in the 1970's, there seemed to be a return to wood stoves for home heating purposes, and it was interesting to me the amount of knowledge that had been lost in the art of building fires, using dampers to control the fire and heat, and choosing different kinds of wood to use for long lasting fires. Several wood stove manufacturers had sprung into business offering some rather common cast iron stoves at space age prices. But there were a few stove companies that never discontinued making them, and those units were reliable, attractive, and safe. This was especially true of stoves from other countries where heating with these units in the seventies was still a part of their lifestyle.

Stoves using wood or sometimes coal when it could be afforded were very much a part of my growing up years. Wood piles in the back yard looked like a couple of Indian teepees and smelled of fresh oak and hickory. During the heating season, the piles would diminish a few sticks at a time till along in May when they would be nearly all gone. If the winter had been especially cold, then some extra had to be cut to fill out the season. For a time, a wood cook stove was used for preparing meals, even in the summer, but finally that gave way to a kerosene stove.

In the front room of our house on Schaad Creek in Hickory Hollow was a heavy cast iron stove called a Heatrola. A few small openings in the door were covered with Micca and allowed a person to see the flames licking around inside. Some of the firelight seeped out and played on the opposite wall. It was pleasant and comforting to watch along with the warm sounds of a fire burning.

My older brother Jack and I came home from school one winter evening and found a note from Mom and Dad saying not to worry, and that they would be home in an hour or so. Jack and I thought the least we could do was to have supper ready when they arrived home. We had limited knowledge of cooking but that didn't bother us a bit. Jack sent me out for a few sticks of firewood while he lit a kerosene lamp and went looking through the kitchen for something to fix. By the time I got back in the house, he had found some morning biscuits and decided that biscuits and gravy would be just the ticket for supper. The Heatrola heating stove in the front room still had some fire in it, so we added some wood and put the big cast iron skillet on top. It was a pretty tall stove—at least to me—and I couldn't see anything that Jack was doing on top.

He kept telling me to go get this and go get that. Finally, when I had a chance, I pulled in a kitchen chair to stand on. I pulled it right up to the Heatrola to see what Jack was putting in the skillet. It looked like he was fixing to make the gravy. He asked me how much grease to use. Heck, I didn't know but we agreed to put in quite a bit and then we added flour just like Mom did. Jack gave me a spoon and said to keep stirring. He knew that Mom always stirred a lot when she made gravy. It didn't look quite right so Jack put in another handful of flour and told me once again to keep stirring.

By now, the fire was crackling right along and getting pretty warm on the front of my bib overalls. Jack closed the damper. He knew all about stoves, and so I kept right on stirring. Then

Jack retrieved a jar of milk from the cool back porch. At the right moment, he added it to our active mixture, carefully chewing his tongue in the corner of his mouth. The gravy calmed down some. There were lumps in it but we stood in complete confidence that this was to be some of the best gravy ever made. I stirred on as Jack added salt, pepper, and a little more milk. Some dribbled on to the inner workings of the stove and made an awful smell. I paid little mind to that, now having some trouble stirring. The gravy was getting awfully thick so Jack added more milk, but it soon stiffened up again and the lumps were still with us. The skillet was full and getting awfully hot.

About then, we heard the Model A Ford come into the driveway. It was time to remove our gravy from the Heatrola. Jack got a potholder from the kitchen and just as he lifted the heavy skillet, spilling only a little of the contents down the front of the stove, Mom and Dad came through the door. As a look of surprise came across their faces, Jack and I stood there with our best smiles of proud accomplishment. Supper was almost ready.

Ungiven Gift

The Frenches walked everywhere from their home in the hollow. They had walked the two miles up the west hollow to Uncle George's and Aunt Daisy's for Thanksgiving dinner. Dave walked miles on his trap line every other day. It was an easy walk through the timber to Frank Warner's for eggs, even in the wintertime.

It was 1939, a time when shortages and the doing-without of the Great Depression were very much a part of recent memory. At the same time, there was uneasiness as nations came closer and closer to a major war.

Now in the depth of December, Dave and Marie told the kids that it was the night for the Christmas program at Hickory Church, just over the hill a mile or so. The kids were eager and soon were dressed in their Sunday best. They put on their overshoes. Dave carried the lantern; Marie carried the youngest child. The older boys were big enough to walk on their own. It was cold enough to see their breath as they began their walk over the hill.

The people of Hickory precinct had a strong faith, and they gathered in the hillside church a few evenings before Christmas to sing praises and celebrate the season and the birth of the baby Jesus.

The Frenches walked into the churchyard. Dave blew out the lantern and set it by the church door. The light shining through the stained-glass windows helped make it a magic evening. The bell rang and rang in the winter air, and soon there was singing louder than anyone had ever heard. The well-to-do, the poor, and the in-between all stood shoulder to shoulder, praying, giving thanks, and singing that December night. The great Christmas tree, some ten feet high, was trimmed and lit with electric lights. Many of the homes in the community were without electricity, so it was a sight to behold for those bright-eyed children.

There was the usual program with Mr. Schaad, the superintendent, speaking in his strong, gravelly voice, "Recitation by Paul Kirchner," "Recitation by Betty Lou Kissinger," "A musical number by Leona Jane Tibbs," and "A Recitation by Jackie David French." And so the evening went on till the magic moment when sleigh bells could be heard outside. Soon good old St. Nick came bursting through the door shouting, "Merry Christmas! Merry Christmas!" He had gifts for all of the children. Santa, with a few helpers, began calling out children's names and handing out gifts. Some were wrapped in fancy papers and tied with ribbons and bows of all colors. He soon emptied his bag, and the big pile of presents under the tree began to dwindle till finally all the name tags had been read.

With a "Ho! Ho! Ho!" old St. Nick wished a Merry Christmas to everyone assembled, waved goodbye, and started his journey back to the North Pole.

But one boy of six years had gone unnoticed. He received no gift. Of all the names called, none was his. He couldn't believe it. Tears as big as raindrops welled in his eyes. He had studied hard in school; he had given his recitation in the best manner he knew how. He thought that he had been a good boy. But no gifts. The only thing he had was a lump in his throat so big he couldn't even eat from the package of candy that everyone received.

He and his family – Mom, Dad, and assorted brothers – left the church and started their walk home. Dad carried the lantern and the youngest child. Everyone had a hold of someone else's hand as the family sloshed along over the half-frozen, muddy road. It was then that Mother began to ask, "Well, what did you get?" to one child and then another.

One child, through quivering lips, replied, "Nothing."

"What?" she said. "Nothing? Well, what on earth? Here, your brother got two things. He can't read and you can, so take his book. Is that OK?"

The book was Thornton W. Burgess' "Old Mother West Wind." The boy had finally received a gift, but it just wasn't the same.

A few days later, the family celebrated their own Christmas with gift giving and a wild game dinner and a generally good and happy time. But the boy kept thinking somewhere in that valley was a gift that wasn't given. Somewhere a gift was wrapped and ready but somehow had been misplaced. Maybe it was lost before it got to the church, but where could it be?

Now World War II is over, and the Great Depression of the 1930s is only mentioned in history. Thornton W. Burgess's "Old Mother West Wind" received that December night rests on a shelf not far from Hickory Church. The families of Hickory precinct have grown and scattered, but somewhere near, there is still an ungiven gift.

Pink Valentine, Red Face

February is the month of the valentine and I think Valentine's Day is well placed. February is a good time to get our minds onto something besides the dreary winter days and how much more it costs each year to survive.

I can't remember the first valentine I ever got nor can I recall the first one I ever sent, but more than likely, it all happened in the first grade at Hickory School. There were only two of us in that grade, Norma Jean and me. When I came out of Hickory Hollow there in September to attend school, she was the first thing I laid eyes on. Pretty as a picture, wearing a plaid dress and a bow in her hair, she was bright-eyed and smart as a whip. That, of course, made me try harder in my reading and writing. So I owe Norma Jean quite a bit for helping me get off to a good start in school.

As Valentine's Day approached, Mom bought an economy package of School Days penny valentines from the Ben Franklin store for my brother and me to exchange with our schoolmates. I probably sorted through them and found a special one for Norma Jean.

And then there was an older girl that sat beside me named Betty. She often wore a skirt with real little pleats all the way around. She was shaped rather well as I recall. Betty liked to stand on the steps of the schoolhouse and spin round and round till the skirt would fly nearly straight out. It was very entertaining till Miss Taylor, the teacher, caught her doing it. That put a stop to that twirling and took the silly grin off the faces of us boys. Betty had to "stay in" a few recesses for displaying such behavior. And I suppose, with all things considered, I probably picked out a valentine for her that was a little special.

When I came back to Hickory to begin my third grade amid the smell of books, pencils, crayons, and new denim overalls, Betty wasn't there and Norma Jean had moved out of my life forever. To this day, I've never found out where she went or what her family ever did.

There were a few new faces to take their places, but no one ever matches the importance of the first classmate you had. One of the new families had a girl named Leona who was older than I was, but she took a liking to me, much to my embarrassment. She promptly nicknamed me "Biscuit Butt" which didn't do a whole lot to win my heart. I turned the reddest when it came time to choose-up sides for some game, and she'd yell out, "We want 'Biscuit Butt' on our side." I'd cross the playing field, staring at the ground but grinning. We usually won, too. I was a pretty fast runner for a little guy. I had to be to outrun Leona. For all the ribbing I took from her, I still thought she was alright and saw to it that I printed extra neat in writing my name on her valentine that year.

We moved out of Hickory Precinct in the early forties. We then became a part of the Cottonwood School District. It was a small school, and for a time there were only six students attending with four of them from our family. We had an excellent teacher, and as the school year got underway, three more boys walked out of the timber to the south and became a part of our school family. It was a ho-hum learning experience with everything going along on schedule. The school was made up mostly of boys except for my younger twin sisters who were just now beginning.

When we returned after Christmas vacation there was another seat filled. The teacher introduced Sally to us. What a difference she made. Every boy could now jump a little higher, run a little faster, and comb his hair a little longer. Fox and the Goose became exciting, as did the other games. She brought a new way to choose up sides with a "one potato, two potato, three potato, four." She was really something else.

Valentine's Day came pretty quickly and I was now along in the sixth grade and had spending money of my own. I knew this Sally girl was going to get something pretty nice if I could afford it. And the other boys were saying the same thing. So on the next trip to town, Mom, of course, bought the economy package of penny valentines for the usual exchange. I had brought along seven cents of my own money. When I got a chance, I sauntered off to Woolworth's Five and Dime to find just the right valentine. Boy, they had some pretty ones. Some were frilly and had all the wrong words. I found one for five cents that had a pink envelope. The verse was a little on the mushy side, but the card was just what I thought Sally would like. I paid the nickel. All afternoon, I kept the pretty valentine with the pink envelope inside my coat so as not to get any wrinkles in it, and at the same time keep it secret from everyone.

On Valentine's Day, I signed my special pink valentine, and put it inside my coat and off to school we went. All the way there, the valentine got heavier and heavier. "Maybe I shouldn't have gotten such a nice one," I thought. "What will the other kids think? I'll throw it away. Then I won't have to worry about it. But then Sally wouldn't get any from me at all." I trudged on to school with the pink envelope getting bigger and bigger.

When we got there, we gave all our valentines to the teacher to put in the box. When she came to the pink one, she said, "Oh my, what a pretty one here. I wonder what lucky girl is going to get this." I turned red and wished I were someplace else.

That was the longest morning I ever put in because the exchange wasn't till after dinner. I still wasn't sure I had done the right thing, but those other boys were going to get her fancy ones, too. Maybe mine wouldn't stand out so much. The teacher began by calling us all round the library table. Then she emptied the box. There, among that pile of skinny little penny valentines was one pink envelope. Gee, it looked big and important. Sally saw her name on it and excitedly reached for it. The teacher handed it to her. She opened it and read the verse. Then she skipped up and down the aisle saying, "I got the prettiest valentine" over and over. I sat there red-faced in my bib overalls, trying to get smaller and smaller, and wishing I could crawl into a crack in the floor as everyone asked, "Who's it from? Who's it from?"

I don't remember much else except that I collected my valentines from well meaning classmates. Even a skinny one from Sally. I left school just a little early so I wouldn't have to walk with the other boys.

It was an embarrassing experience, but if I had it all to do over again, I'd probably do the same thing.

I've never gotten over the habit of sending valentines, and I will send out a few again this year.

Roy and his classmate in the second grade at Hickory School.

Potato Harvest

I went out to dig some potatoes the other evening after supper and could hardly get the fork into the ground. This has been one of the driest months on record. But what few hills I was able to dig up showed some pretty nice potatoes. Before I harvest the rest of them, I'm going to wait for a rain to loosen the ground.

Years back, Dad and Grandpa planted a good sized patch of potatoes across the creek from our house there in Hickory Hollow. It was something they did every year, but that year they planted a special potato called an Early Ohio. For some reason or other they were to be the finest potatoes ever grown. It could be the reason was that my great grandpa came from Ohio. Therefore, anything with Ohio associated with it was the best.

When the potato plants were up a ways, maybe ten inches high, the potato bugs came and started riddling the leaves. Jack and I had the job of keeping the bugs off the plants. To do this, we carried a bucket and a stick. We placed the bucket on the ground and leaned it towards the plant. Then we took the short stick and shook the plant toward the bucket. You'd be surprised how many of those little orange bugs fell in. By the time we finished the patch, we had maybe a half inch of bugs in the bucket. We took them back to the house to show Grandpa what a fine job we'd done. He was always pleased. He poured about a cup of kerosene in each bucket and that was the end of the pesky leaf eaters.

The plants set on blooms and Grandpa continued to hoe and tend that potato patch. Next to smoking his pipe, Grandpa enjoyed hoeing with his favorite three corner hoe. Finally, the plants were laid by to finish making potatoes.

When an early autumn came that year, the Early Ohios did everything they were expected to do. The potatoes were four and five to the hill, smooth and round, and had good flavor. It was a bumper crop.

We had a Model A Ford at the time. The Model A car could be adapted to do most anything. Sacks of corn and bales of hay could be put on the fenders next to the hood. Ladders and lumber, poles and bedsprings could be put on top. If you could get it on, you could haul it.

Dad built a platform of wood that fit over the back bumpers and made a small truck bed about three feet by four feet wide, and that was how Dad was going to haul potatoes from the patch, across the creek, and to the cellar by the house. We had to go out of the driveway down the road a hundred yards, cross the bridge, and then turn down into the potato patch. Grandpa dug the potatoes out while Dad and we kids put the potatoes into gunny sacks. When we had enough sacks for a load on the Model A, we made a trip to the cellar. Our whole family was having a good time getting in the potato harvest.

On one trip, I just slipped up and sat on the rear platform with the sacks of potatoes. Dad said, "If you're going to ride there, you be careful." He drove out of the potato patch and onto the road with the little Ford riding pretty low behind.

Like any kid, I dragged my feet in the dust as we went along, with me facing backward as the car went forward. And then I thought I'd just step off. I'd seen people step off moving street cars in Peoria and it looked like fun. So I just eased up and slipped off the edge of the platform, expecting to step onto the road. Boy, did I get a surprise! When my feet hit the ground, I did three backward somersaults in that deep clay dust. As soon as I stopped rolling, I snapped to my feet as if nothing had happened and went walking right along. Dad turned into the driveway just as I was emerging from the cloud of dust. He stopped, and with a concerned look on his face asked, "Did you fall off back there?"

Just as quick, I answered, "Nope. Just wanted to walk," and kept right on walking toward the cellar.

I had dust in my shirt, my shoes, my hair, and my eyes. I was dust from one end to the other and a whole lot smarter about how to step off a moving Model A Ford.

Fall of Forty-One

In 1941 our family there in Hickory Hollow had seen a very good summer come to a close. The garden of rich timber soil had produced all kinds of fruits and vegetables in abundance. Mom, with all her energy, had canned and cold packed enough food stuff to last us through the winter.

Carpenter work had been good for Dad and his brother, Elmo. Work had been steady. The Depression was lessening and wages had climbed to a respectable level again. I remember Dad coming home one evening and before he ever got into the house, telling Mom that they were able to raise their wages from forty to forty-five cents an hour. "Just think, Marie," he said, "that's four dollars and fifty cents a day." Dad worked ten-hour days then.

It was soon after that Dad traded off a much worn Model A Ford for a shiny black 1936 Chevy coach. It had a six-cylinder engine, chrome hub caps, and Firestone tires. Fancy upholstery was on the doors and seats, and there wasn't a hole in it anywhere. It was better than anything we had ever dreamed of.

Times were good at the moment, but there was war brewing in other parts of the world. Grandpa read the paper and talked of bombers being built and troops being trained. Hitler was razing Europe, and storm clouds of war appeared on every horizon.

Mom had three brothers still living in Wisconsin, all at prime ages, should a draft begin. More often Dad, Grandpa, and Mom gathered around the table radio at news time. "Ah, yes. There is good news tonight," Gabriel Heatter, the news commentator, would begin. What followed was not good news at all.

The troubles of the world were getting deeper and we kids could sense it. At school we heard talk of brothers and uncles enlisting in the service—the Army, Navy, Marines, or the Army Air Force. And we, in turn, at our minor ages chose to be airplane pilots, or wanted to drive a battleship, or maybe a tank.

Occasionally we stopped our play in the schoolyard and strained our ears to hear several airplanes approaching. Later we came to know them as squadrons. Sometimes they were small and fast with only one engine. Other times they had two or four engines. We stood in awe and silently counted them—16, 17, 18, 19, 20, and so on. Not a kid made a sound but stood, mouth open, looking up. After they had all passed, we went back to our playing but a little more reserved. Maybe someone we knew, some son from our valley, was flying one of those war planes.

At supper, Mom and Dad talked of shortages that might occur as the war became more active. Gasoline was already being rationed in the east. Our ships were being torpedoed in the Atlantic. As if the country were not suffering enough, John L. Lewis, powerful Union leader of the coal miners, picked October to call a strike in direct defiance of President Roosevelt. That's one thing that wouldn't bother us all that much. Dad and Grandpa had the woodpile ricked up high in the back yard.

Churchill's voice came wavering over our battery radio and promised that Britain would join the United States in an hour should we become involved in a war with Japan. But we were trying to avoid war. I was in the third grade at the time and pictured in my mind that I would use the old single shot Marlin rifle that hung above the kitchen door if I had to do any shooting. At supper, I asked Dad if there was going to be any shooting and fighting around the house. Would the Germans or Japs come that close? "No, no," he said. "The war is far, far off." But I knew he was concerned, and it wasn't about the war coming to Hickory. What would he do? How would he handle it if he had to go to a far away war? He'd have to leave everything he'd built there and his wife, whose family was in Wisconsin. With his children, the three boys all growing strong, and the twin girls just babies, what would the family do?

So just as the depression was put behind us and things began to look better, other dark closets of unknown contents were opening.

***

Winter came early to our hollow in the fall of forty-one. As the angles of the sun lowered, the days grew noticeably shorter. By the time Jack and I returned home from school, our yard was in near darkness. The last rays of the sunlight over our heads were just lifting from the tree tops in the east hillside pasture. The cool dampness closed in fast as the yellow light from the kerosene lamps spilled out of the windows to erase a little of the darkness. The Heatrola was banked full of wood and the blue smoke from the chimney formed a cloud that moved slowly with the heaviness of cold, still air.

When we came into the house, Mom was frying some kind of wild game—rabbit, squirrel, or quail—that Dad had killed that day. From the hillside cellar came potatoes and vegetables that gave us more to eat than we could ever hope for. Dad had just come in with fresh milk from the Jersey cow. He took off his coat and overshoes and put them by the kitchen range to keep them warm.

Suppertime was always special for us kids because it was the one time each day that our whole family was together, and it was the big meal of the day. The day's events were discussed. My older brother, Jack, six year old Billy John and I sat with our backs to the windows toward the creek. Dad sat on the side of the table, while Mom sat on the end closest to the stove and cupboards. The twin girls, who were the youngest, sat closest to Mom. They still needed a little help at mealtime. That made seven of us around the table.

After supper, Grandpa came from his room, bringing the paper for Dad to read and laid it on the rocker in the front room. He lit his pipe and, recounting the printed news, said that John Lewis was about ready to let miners go back to work, that we had just lost a big ship in the Atlantic, that a submarine had sunk it, and that from now on, we were going to arm our ships. My third grade mind wondered what a submarine was.

The war continued to pick up steam. Places like Africa, Indo-China, Guiana, and Poland were mentioned in nightly newscasts. President Roosevelt, Sir Winston Churchill, and the League of Nations were in constant communication trying to avert the worst. Our breakfast cereal boxes had all kinds of war slogans printed on them as well as ways to identify enemy planes, tanks, and ships. Uncle Dick and Aunt Dot worked in a defense plant in Alton making bullets. They told of all the windows being painted blue in the factory, and I asked why that was done. Uncle Dick told me it was so a German or Jap bomber coming over at night would not be able to see the lights of the factory.

At school our teacher, a stern Miss Taylor, had a new phonograph record to play on the Victrola. It was "God Bless America" sung by a lady named Kate Smith. Miss Taylor played it every morning and stood beside the Victrola, in reverence, till the needle made the last scratch. Within a week we knew the words by heart, and soon she had every child singing along with the record. "Stand beside her and guide her, through the night, with a light from above." The song and the flag raising each morning became a time of emotion and great feeling as to what America stood for. It was patriotism to the limit. And we kids there, some twenty of us in that one room schoolhouse, were true Americans from the toes of our holey socks to the tips of our runny noses.

By now the war had touched our valley. Most of us knew someone who had already left home to fight a people in another land far away. Occasionally, we would learn that someone we knew was killed or missing at sea and would not turn the soil of our valley again.

Because we had plenty right there in the neighborhood, because we had plenty at home, and were safe and warm, we thought again of how fortunate we were. So as Thanksgiving came in the fall of forty-one and was celebrated at church and school and home, we said an extra prayer.

***

As Hitler laid waste to towns and villages across Europe and German submarines sank our merchant ships in the Atlantic, the United States was edging toward an all out war faster than we knew. In preparation, the U. S. was building ordinance plants with any kind of labor force available. Munitions plants were pressed to work around the clock. Men building planes and working in shipyards worked two shifts, slept for a shift, and then returned to work again. But that was all in other places like Rock Island, Baraboo, Illiopolis, and St. Louis. There at Hickory, the timbered flats and prairie knolls, the intoxicating musk of rotting grass in an aging autumn, and the heady teas of curing willow leaves put the war far, far away from our Hollow.

Early winter helped furnish a bumper crop of healthy fur-bearing animals. Dad and the Cox boys were out almost every night to exercise the hounds. My brother and I snuggled warm in our bedroom that measured ten feet by twelve feet, and strained our ears to hear the hounds run, and sometimes we did. Much later the hunters would come in with a coon, possum, or an occasional skunk that Mom could smell a full hour before they arrived. Dad had a trap line to run by day. Between the traps and nighttime hunting, he soon had a barn loft hanging full of drying pelts.

Every two weeks George would drive out from town to our place there in the Hollow, climb into the barn loft with Dad, chew tobacco, spit, cuss, and bargain for the furs. It was an education to my third grade ears to hear them haggle as to what was prime and what was common. It was always the same, but they'd come to terms and settlement would be made. Mr. Griffin would return to town with the back seat of his Ford car weighted down with the stinking skins, and Dad had money in his pocket.

The price of fur was rising as the war effort gained momentum. More soldiers and pilots needed warm clothing and fur was filling a special need.

It was now the first of December. The ground had frozen an inch or so, and then thawed. Cold rains came and washed the clay till the quagmire of Hickory Road went on forever. With so many shortages of manpower, fuel, and materials, the township roads got very little attention. Already Dad had gotten the fancy '36 Chevy stuck a time or two. He hated that. He was so proud of that car.

The shorter days grew damp and bone chilling cold, but we children had plenty to wear with hand-me-down or made over coats. Mom loved to sew and would rather sew than eat. She pedaled that Singer sewing machine through yards and yards of cloth, making about anything the family needed as it grew in size and number. Sometimes it was pretty cool weather before she got the last coat ready to wear, but we never suffered.

One morning as we prepared to go off to school little brother Billy John, who was in the first grade, wasn't feeling so good. That afternoon, he was still complaining of his belly hurting, and Jack carried him home on his back. The next day Jack and I attended school alone. When we returned home, we learned that our folks had taken Billy John to see Doc Felt. Doc said he had a little trouble with his bowel "as all little boys do" and gave Mom a laxative for him. But Billy John remained a pretty sick little boy, holding his lower stomach and crying a low, sobbing cry. He slept some that night but still wouldn't eat any breakfast.

When Jack and I got home from school the next evening, our folks were pretty concerned. Their child hadn't eaten in a couple of days, and Dad and Mom hadn't slept much either. Dad said "If he's not better by morning, Marie, we'd better try to get him to the doctor's again."

Grandpa came into the room, shifted his pipe around in his mouth and said, "By Gosh, Davey, I don't like the looks of the boy."

It was a restless and uneasy night for everyone. Mom, with all her concern for the little one, rushed Jack and me off to school early the next morning. We walked up Hickory Hill over the rutted and frozen road with patches of ice covering mud holes and water.

HICKORY ROAD

While the ground was still frozen, Dad got the Chevy out of the garage. Mom bundled up Billy John. The little boy was hot with fever, pale, and hardly made a sound. Whether they could get to town and to the doctor's office without getting stuck was another matter. Leaving Grandpa to look after the twin girls, they headed out with Billy John.

Dad was a good mud driver and pushed the Chevy hard in low and second gear, bouncing in one rut and out to another, fighting the wheel and trying to pick the best way through without bumping any more than they had to. With each jolt of the car, Billy John let out a week scream. Mom tried to protect him as much as she could. The wash-out at Warner's Curve nearly shook the car apart, but they made it through and were on the flat ground with only a few more miles to go. It was a tense time, but they finally reached the new hard road and the paved streets of Virginia. They soon pulled the mud spattered Chevy into a parking place beside Doc Felt's long, black Buick.

Mom got out with her whimpering child and Dad, weary for sleep, opened the office door. They came into the waiting room and said nothing. Doc Felt leaned out of the examining room and said, "I'll be with you in a minute, Davey." But then he looked at Billy John's face among the blankets. He walked over and pulled the blanket back. His eyes firmed. He touched the boy's face with his hand and muttered something.

Doc Felt went to the telephone, lifted the receiver and gave the crank a turn. "Hilma," he said, "Can you get me Our Saviors right quick." There was a pause. Then he said, "This is Doc Felt in Virginia. I've got a little boy here. He's pretty sick. I'll be there in a few minutes. Be ready for me."

***

Doc Felt put the telephone receiver back on the hook. He went to the examination room and told whoever was in there that he'd have to be gone for awhile. Dad and Mom, with all the caring that parents could have, knew that something was pretty serious for anyone to go to Our Savior's Hospital in Jacksonville.

Doc put on his rumpled hat, scarf, and heavy dark overcoat. He took Mom's arm, opened the door and said, "Davey, you and Marie sit in back. This will be a pretty fast trip. Don't worry. Just sit tight." Mom and Dad, with Billy John, got in the Buick while Doc warmed the engine.

Buicks were known for being fast road cars that handled well, especially the 1938 model that Doc had. The long, eight cylinder engine with dual carburetors had plenty of power. Doc backed the car out onto the brick street and headed south out of town. Dad got a hold of the side strap with one hand and pulled Mom and the very sick little boy close to him with the other. The Buick was warming up and Doc was letting it out. Sixty, sixty-five, seventy miles an hour. The car was heavy and held to the road. From the back seat, it looked like it was forty feet to the front of the long, shiny hood. Doc, sitting erect and at full attention, had the wheel of the fine car and was doing his best for Billy John. Dad never liked speed, but this time he didn't care. The Buick moved up to eighty on the Literberry flat and hummed as if it had more to go. Doc kept a steady hand on the wheel and a firm foot on the floor and pushed the big black car on south. Surely each minute counted.

They came into the north edge of Jacksonville a full sixty miles an hour and made straight way for Our Savior's Hospital. Nurses were waiting at the rear entrance and gave silent greetings as they came through the door. Doc talked to them in a low voice, turned to Mom and Dad, and led them into and examining room with several other doctors. The medical staff pressed and felt the crying child. "Terrible fever," one said. "He'll never survive the fever."

Doc Felt called Mom and Dad to one side and said, "We're pretty sure it's his appendix. It must have burst. Whatever it is, we must do something quick. We'll have to operate. He's only got a few hours if we don't, and Davey, it doesn't look very good."

Mom and Dad, with tired ashen faces, looked at each other and said, "O.K."

"We'll do our best," replied Doc.

"I know you will, Doc," Dad answered.

With that, they wheeled Billy John away on a stretcher, a small body, grey and limp. He was in the hands of Doc Felt, a few surgeons, and God.

Jack and I didn't know all this was going on. I don't remember what we did that night after school. I'm not sure whether Dad came home then or the next day. It could be that somebody came and stayed with us. But we soon learned that Billy John had been awfully sick and was taken to a hospital and operated on and that he had come through the operation, still hanging to a very thin thread of life, which was some kind of a miracle. He had had an appendicitis. It swelled and ruptured, spreading a poisonous gangrene infection throughout his little body. His fever had been 106° when they brought him into the hospital, and they didn't know how long it had been that way. They figured that in about two more hours, it would have been too late. I'm sure Dad, in his waiting times, wondered about the big bump on Warner's Curve. Could it have burst the appendix? What if they had gotten stuck for an hour or two?

A new miracle drug was being tried in the armed forces, but it wasn't used very much in private practice, except in special cases. This was a special case and Doc Felt wanted to use it. It promised to be a real infection fighter, and Billy John was filled with infection. Doc called for the use of the drug. It was called penicillin. Dad tried to pronounce it but couldn't get it right. It didn't matter as long as it helped his little boy.

Mom moved into the hospital, living in a chair beside Billy John's bed. She was conscience of his every breath—coming in—going out. How beautiful it was. The days passed slowly. The little boy showed some improvement. His color was coming back, his movements more positive. And Doc Felt kept a special interest. The miracle drug was working, but Doc admitted later that God had surely played the stronger part.

***

With Mom staying at Billy John's hospital bedside, life was a little different in the hollow for the rest of us. Dad was doing alright at home acting as Mother, Dad, housekeeper, and cook. Grandma Dena came out a few days a week and an old family friend, Mrs. Thomas, helped out, too. The routine we practiced strengthened us and helped put a few braces back in our shaken little world. We were going to survive, and relatives, friends and neighbors all played a part and provided a strength.

At school, we put away our turkeys and pilgrims and were cutting out Christmas trees from green construction paper. We made paper chains out of different colored paper and stuck them together with a sticky white paste. We sang "Jingle Bells" and an occasional Christmas carol along with "God Bless America."

The war was still on our minds but Christmas was coming, too. Surely Mom and Billy John would be home by then.

Dad still had a trap line to look after. It was our only source of income. It was not an easy time for him. He made trips to the hospital as often as he could to see his wife and child. The boy was still fighting a fever. He couldn't eat any solid food but seemed to be winning. The little country boy was tough. Jack and I still had a little brother.

The weather took a turn for the worse. The snow had melted, and when the temperature dropped, a hard crust froze on the top. Most of Dad's traps were frozen in. No game moved. There was no need to run the traps and, of course, money stopped coming in.

Many times Dad stood alone with his back to the cook stove, his hands carried on the bib of his overalls. He scratched the frosty windows and looked to a landscape of frozen creeks and barren trees. Maybe it came to him in those periods of thought that the backwoods may not be the best place to live and raise a family. He'd been to Peoria, worked at Caterpillar Tractor, and saw the seamy side of life in the crowded city. It was neither a place for him nor his children. The purity was in the country, the hills and valleys where he and his father before him had been raised. But times were changing. Now with the war, the awful roads and an economy that depended more on the dollar, maybe there was a better place. Still he couldn't get anything to come clear in his mind.

December 7, 1941 came. The Japanese with many war planes bombed Pearl Harbor and other United States territories in the Pacific. Many, many of our battleships were sunk and unknown thousands of our service men perished in that one awful day. On December 8, the United States declared war on Japan. On December 11, Germany and Italy declared war on the United States. On December 19, Congress passed a bill extending the draft to those 20 to 44 years of age.

Dad was 39 years old, had a wife, twin daughters, and three sons, one very sick in the hospital. He had a hundred traps frozen in the ice, and maybe ten dollars in his pocket. Hickory Road, our only connection to the outside world, was washed, rutted and frozen till it was impassable by car.

Dad saw his few dollars dwindle as the days ticked off toward Christmas. He worried about the hospital bill. My God, what was it going to cost? Six or eight dollars a day and it had been over three weeks since Billy John went in. How would he ever pay it?

Dad perfected two things during that time—prayer and potato soup. Both were very beneficial to our well being. One may have been an answer to the other. He made one of the best pots of potato soup there ever was. Rich yellow butter floated around the edges above onions and potatoes, tender and tasty. We had it about every third night for supper there by lamplight, and we always looked forward to it. During our together times, we found a brighter side. We did all right.

School occupied me and Jack as we listened to the upper grade students reading the Christmas carols while others had the agony of memorizing "Twas the Night Before Christmas" and other poems. Along with our studies, we continued with our paper decorations and a little singing. The last day of classes before Christmas vacation finally arrived. A Christmas party during the afternoon included a meager gift exchange, a few songs, and generally a good time.

Jack and I hadn't seen Mom or Billy John for a long time. Each time Dad had a chance to go over to the hospital, he brought word back that Mom missed us very much and would be home as soon as she could. Billy John was doing very well. Only a few days before, Doc Felt had visited the little boy. He carried a walnut and a nutcracker in his pocket. He cracked the nut and picked out the meat for Billy John to eat. "Here, Sonny. How does this taste to you?" Doc asked.

Billy John smiled and said it tasted good. Doc told Mom, "Pay special attention to him. See if he experiences any pain during the next twenty-four hours. If he doesn't, then the appendix has healed completely and he can begin taking solid foods." It was a great day. Billy John was on his way.

During Christmas vacation Jack and I went to Aunt Etta's to stay. Etta wasn't really our aunt, but our family affectionately gave her that title. If we ever had anybody that was like a second mother to us, it was Aunt Etta.

She and her husband Olin, along with two grown sons and a daughter, lived on a black sand farm about a mile down river and over the Sixth Street levee from Beardstown. We always enjoyed it there and were making the best of it again, even though the move scattered our family even more.

Aunt Etta got up at an ungodly early hour, milked four cows and delivered the milk on a route in Beardstown. She'd bottle it up in the morning, Jack and I would put it in the Ford car, and off we'd go with Etta driving, telling stories, or singing some song about half out loud. We looked forward to the milk route. It seemed never to be the same and always interesting. She filled our days as best she could, sometimes hitching a mule to a string of sleds and galloping off over snowy fields and roads with us kids hanging on for dear life.

But Etta had a load to carry, too. She had two boys at prime service age. One was already reading everything he could get his hands on about flying. With the boys gone, she would have to carry that much more.

But most of the days were good. We knew that Christmas was near and Billy John and Mom would be coming home soon.

Other days began with melancholy crowding in and staying like an unwelcome guest till nighttime came. Then we went to bed in strange rooms under unfamiliar covers with lumps in our throats, listening to river boats go chuga chuga chuga through the night. Missing everyone and everything familiar, we wondered if we'd ever be all back together again in our home in the Hollow.

***

One morning a few days before Christmas, Dad woke up slowly and sensed that something had changed during the night. He looked out the window to see heavy fog filling the snow-covered hollow. Surely the weather was warming. Maybe by evening the traps would be free of ice.

With the warming trend, all the animals that had been holed up would now be out moving, foraging and feeding in the creeks and fields. It was a day of anticipation for Dad, not knowing for sure what the next day would bring. But if prayers were answered, he'd know it early next morning.

So that night Dad slept restlessly, thinking of his wife in Jacksonville with a little boy that was getting well, of the older two boys at Aunt Etta's and the twins being cared for by Grandma, of Christmas only a few days away, and of the lack of money for gifts or anything else. By five o'clock in the morning, he could stay in bed no longer. He got up, fired up the stove with chunks of oak, dressed, fixed a hurried breakfast, put on his boots and hunting coat, and off he went to his traps.

He approached the first trap down the east branch of Schaad Creek. He held up the kerosene lantern, straining to see by the dim light through the chill damp darkness of that morning. Two narrow set shining eyes reflected back at him. A mink! He'd caught a mink, a beautiful twenty-dollar mink. Dad's spirits were more than alive then. He could hardly keep from running from trap to trap.

He moved on in a near trot, up the creek, across fallen corn, to hill sets for fox and wolf. He returned home in the afternoon, weighted down with two minks, a red fox, four raccoons, and a scrawny muskrat, nearly seventy dollars worth of fur. He knew prayers were answered.

Dad didn't take time to skin the fur but put them in the Chevy and drove out of the hollow before the road got completely thawed. He went right to the fur buyer's. George came out of the house as Dad unloaded the fur on the snow. "George," Dad said, "I had a good catch this morning. Didn't take time to skin it. Wanted to get to town while I could still get over the road."

George didn't look at the fur but asked, "How's the boy, Davey?"

"I'm on my way over there now. He's much better. Going to do all right. May be home in a few days," Dad answered.

George took his foot and rolled the fresh caught fur around, spit to one side and said, "They all look like prime pelts to me, Dave. I'll give you top dollar for 'em"

"What about the scrawny rat?" Dad asked.

"You heard what I said, Dave, and if you're a wanting to get on your way, don't worry about skinnin 'em."

Dad didn't know what to think. George counted out seventy-two dollars and fifty cents into Dad's hand. Dad looked old George full in the face and said, "Dammit, George. About the time I get to thinking you're no account, you do something nice like this." Dad reached out and shook his hand. George returned a tight lipped smile.

Dad went to Grandma's there in town, hugged his toddling twin daughters, shaved and cleaned up, bought a tank full of gas and headed for the hospital. It was late afternoon when he got there. Billy John was sitting up in bed eating a good supper. Mom looked rested. He told her the good news, showed her the handful of money and said, "Maybe we can do a little Christmas shopping now."

"Oh, David!" she said. And they gave each other a long hug.

The next morning, they came down to Aunt Etta's to see Jack and me. I was in the front room reading on the floor at the end of the couch, somewhat out of sight as the door between the rooms was partly open to hide me. Jack was in the kitchen with Etta, and I heard her say, "Jack! Roy Lee! Here come your Mom and Dad."

We hadn't seen Mom for several weeks. That was an awfully long time for Jack and me. We missed her, of course, but kids are pretty flexible and we kept busy. It hadn't been so bad. But when I heard the door slam as they came onto the porch, I felt surprised. "They are really here!" I thought.

I remained on the floor at the end of the couch by the front room door. When Mom and Dad came into the kitchen, I heard their voices and turned to look through the crack in the door between the hinges. There was much hugging and how are you's between Mom and Etta and Dad and Jack and others. Mom looked really pretty. Perhaps she had lost a little weight during her vigil at the hospital. Her clothes were not new but they looked fresh and fit her well. She looked great and so did Dad.

As I watched through the crack in the door, feelings came to me as to how much I had really missed her and I didn't know what to do. In a minute she asked, "Where's Roy Lee?"

Etta said, "Oh, he's around here someplace." As the group moved into the front room, the door pushed open to enclose me a little more, but as Mom's dress went by, I arose from my corner and hugged her around the hips. There wasn't anything I could say, nor could she. But still, a lot was being felt. I may have cried a little.

Just as quickly, the situation became very happy. They told of how fine Billy John was doing, that he was eating well and would be able to come home soon, and of the good luck with the trap line yesterday morning. Mom and Dad said they'd be back for us the next day. We would all be together in the Hollow for Christmas Day. Soon they left for town to buy groceries before going home to start the fires and warm the house. It would be the first time in nearly a month that Mom and Dad would be together with just each other. How good that must have felt.

The next morning they came and picked up Jack and me just as they said they would. That afternoon, they brought Billy John home from the hospital. It was a Christmas to remember. Even though the gifts were meager, our family was coming together again, and more of the Christmas spirit filled our little house that December than in any Christmas I can ever remember. Even yet, it is difficult for me to write about.

No one, of course, would wish for those circumstances again, the prerequisites to that most hallowed Christmas, but everyone searches for that same spirit. Anyone who hasn't been there, anyone that hasn't experienced such things, can never know the feelings. I shall never forget. Two years later, we moved out of the depth of the Hollow and as they say, some leavings must be permanent. It was for me.

In the following seasons when we went to town from our new place on the bottom road, we never went by the old place in the Hollow. Too much of us remained there. But just as leaving the womb and its warmth and security, we all longed for the good years and good times in the Hollow, drinking the water from the earth, eating the food from the soil, and sharing the air with the leaves and grasses. Much of us remained in that place.

Our home in Hickory Hollow.
Schaad Creek runs about twenty yards to the left of the house.

A Blessing of Ducks

The creeks leading to the river along the Sangamon Valley bluffs come winding out of the hills to the south. Those creeks are fed by many clear-water springs trickling from gravel bars along the banks. Years ago during my childhood, our family of seven lived on such a creek, Schaad Creek, and it carried away the watershed of Hickory Hollow toward the Sangamon River.

One December in the early 1940's was an especially difficult time. Mid-December found us with roads nearly impassable by hub deep mud. That was soon followed by a bitter freeze. Few cars of that era would start under such conditions, and those that did found the frozen, rutted surfaces impossible to negotiate. My older brother Jack, younger brother Billy, and I were able to walk over the hill to Hickory School, but Mother and the still younger twin sisters were pretty much homebound. Dad was able to get out to his trap line, maybe help a neighbor butcher, or do other odd jobs, but the weather conditions prevented him from practicing his regular trade of carpentry. Add to that the complexities, discouragement, and shortages of a country at war, and you begin to understand the stresses of that long ago winter.

After many days at school doing Christmas things and listening to Bing Crosby sing a brand new song called "White Christmas," we were dismissed for the holiday vacation. We three boys trudged home in anticipation of better things to come.

As we walked up the meandering hill, we could hear the distant chorus of ducks flying overhead. Wave after wave, millions of birds, chattering their duck songs of communication, all flying from the river bottom sloughs of Gumtown and Wilcox Lake to feed on prairie fields of corn. We'd occasionally stop, look upward, and see the low winter sun glinting off quickly beating wings reminding us of twinkling lights. Our breath was very visible in the shadows where we stood.

As we neared our house nestled there beside the creek, snow began to fall, much to the delight of my brothers and me. Snow was a miracle. It came from the heavens and covered the ugliness of rutted roads and turned our rural landscape into a fresh new world. Even as darkness came, we began to see the changing hills and woods.

As our family sat around our supper table in the light of the kerosene lamp, Mother talked of what we might have for Christmas dinner. Plenty of vegetables were tucked away in the root cellar and she baked bread every few days. But what kind of main dish would we be able to have? Dad said that duck and dressing would be mighty fine, but he hadn't had a chance to get any. Maybe he'd be able to go duck hunting in a day or two. Mom thought duck and dressing would be just perfect to go with Wisconsin cranberries.

I made trips to the window, scraped away the frost and shined a flashlight outside. It was still snowing. I kept checking every chance I got. I opened the back door, shining the light toward the woodpile and smokehouse. Dad told me to shut the door and took the flashlight away from me, saying I was going to run the battery down. But I had gotten to see that the snow was getting pretty deep. We were going to have a white Christmas just like Bing Crosby was singing about on the school Victrola.

Later we gathered around the battery radio for the evening news. By some kind of magic, a signal was sifted from the night air by a thin wire stretched from our chimney to the Mulberry tree. Announcer Julian Bentley told of battles and bombings of the war and troubles on the home front. The weather report was not good either. The battery began to fade, but we heard in the lessening voices of a severe winter storm crossing Illinois.

But to me, all else was far away, and I curled up near the Heatrola stove to watch the flames make dancing images on the wall through the isinglass door. The old stove with a bellyful of hardwood made friendly sounds that comforted me. I heard ticks and murmurs and minor wheezes and contented sighs. The pleasant aroma of wood smoke, hot cast-iron, and a little burning dust mixed with the fragrance of the cedar Christmas tree. It was still snowing out and I was secure inside, sitting in a little corner of heaven.

The next morning snow continued to fall, and the wind roared in the treetops on the hill as we began the first day of winter, that time when only short periods of light are given us, followed by long, dark nights. We kids remained in the house till after lunch. By then, Mom needed some space and asked us to go outside for awhile. We went to look down the creek. We looked through snow flakes to our favorite places. Even though it was very cold, we could see open water where springs fed the stream. "Look, Jack," I said excitedly, "there's a duck in the water."

We looked up and down the creek and saw ducks in every space of open water. We looked up into the falling snow and heard ducks and saw ducks flying lower than we'd ever seen them. Ducks were everywhere. We were beyond ourselves in wonder. We three brothers burst into the house, scattering snow everywhere and yelling, "Where's Dad? Where's Dad? There are ducks all over the place!"

Mom told us to get ourselves back outside and said that Dad had walked up through the timber to Mr. Warner's to buy some eggs. As we rushed back out, we saw Dad returning. We ran to him, telling of all the ducks and pointing to the creek. His eyes widened in disbelief. But there were the ducks – mallards, drakes and hens, and pintails and canvasbacks – everywhere.

It was a phenomenon. The bitter cold and driving snowstorm had driven the ducks from the frozen river and sloughs. They sought refuge in the sheltered hollows and open waters of spring-fed creeks.

Dad was a good shot. With the reliable Winchester pump and a few shells, he brought down several ducks while his sons ran in the deep snow to retrieve them. A hundred could have been killed, but he took only a few. We could look forward to a fine Christmas dinner of roast duck and dressing with Mom's favorite Wisconsin cranberries.

What we needed but were unable to get, Providence brought to us. We were happy and thankful for the blessing of ducks. It is a fond Christmas memory that stays with me yet today.

The War Years

We were fishing down at Rawlins' off a sandbar that extended into a bar pit near the Illinois River. It was an autumn day with puffy clouds in the sky placed just right. We watched the lazy current move the willow leaves back and forth. Leaves from the Cottonwood trees fell on the water and went drifting by. We imagined them to be boats and ships sailing away to their destinations on an October day. It was in the fall of 1944, the war years, and I was eleven years old.

The fish weren't biting very well but we fished anyway. It was a pleasant thing to do on a sunny Sunday afternoon. Dad and Olin visited. We three boys were happy to be fishing and close to the water.

In mid-afternoon Etta came walking over the sand levee bare foot and in a hurry. She walked straight to the men. They talked with anxious voices. We kids couldn't hear what they were saying, but it was something serious. Apparently someone had come out from town. This person knew a telegram had arrived at the post office on a Sunday and felt the message was important enough to track down the recipient. The telegram was for Marie French, our mother. She could go to the post office and get it if she could raise the postmaster. Olin knew the postmaster.

Dad told us to keep on fishing and that he'd be back in awhile. He and Olin hurried back to the house. Dad, Mom and Olin got in Olin's Ford car and drove into town to the postmaster's house. He was ready for them. They went together to the post office where he handed Mom the telegram.

With shaking hands she opened it to learn that her brother Sam, an air force bomber pilot, had been shot down over Turkey and was missing in action. All her fears came welling up inside her. The worst had happened.

We kids had given up fishing early in the afternoon. When Mom and Dad and Olin got back from town, we knew something bad had happened. Mom was so quiet and her eyes were red.

We kept to ourselves going home that night in our old Chevy through the deep sand by Treadway's corner, over the Sixth Street levee and on up the bottom road. There was a chill in the air. No one was talking. It was a night we were glad to crawl into bed.

Three weeks passed before we learned that Sam had been captured by the Germans and was in a prisoner of war camp. At least he was alive. We were much relieved. But Mom's brother, Gus, was in the navy and fighting in the Philippines. She worried about him. He wrote now and then, and he wasn't in dangerous fighting.

She had another brother, Babe. He was in the infantry and was in some of the worst battles of all in Europe – Utah Beach, Normandy, the Ardennes, the Rhine River. His platoon would go in and they'd all be killed, all but ten. He would be one of the ten that lived. It was like that in many of his battles. Mom would get a censored letter after the battle was over saying that he was alright, but she worried anyway. She worried that he wouldn't be so lucky the next time.

Christmas was coming. How would she send a Christmas gift to someone in a prisoner of war camp? How would Christmas greetings find their way to the Philippines? How would she send Christmas cheer to someone in a foxhole in Europe? It was a heavy time. The war news in the papers was not good.

One evening we all sat down at the supper table after what had been a difficult day, a short day. It was already dark out and the light from the Aladdin lamp didn't drive the darkness from the corners of the room. We were about to eat – Dad, brothers Jack and Bill, the twin sisters and me with Mom beside me. She had fixed supper but couldn't eat. She stared in thought a moment. Then she put her hands over her face and broke down in tears – quietly at first, then with more intensity. We all put our forks down, Dad, the twins, the brothers, all of us, and we sat there with our heads bowed. It was silent except for Mom's crying. In a little while she composed herself. We all looked up and started eating. We talked little. We realized the load that Mom was carrying. We five kids and Dad were enough, but when you added three brothers in the war to her worries, it was just too much for her to bear.

From that day on each of us in our own way tried to make life easier for Mom. We kids didn't gripe about chores but did them gladly. Mom and I did the dishes. It was fun. She washed, I dried. I looked forward to spending time with Mom. We didn't talk about what we wanted for Christmas. We knew Mom would do the best she could with the money she had.

Going into winter and a new year, we were a family intact. We were all glad for one another, the brothers, and sisters, and Mom and Dad too. The new year would be a better year.

Firecrackers

I was in Winchester the other day. Some kids were setting off firecrackers in a neighborhood lot. They were doing the usual things kids do with firecrackers such as setting them off under tin cans and watching them jump into the air or putting a firecracker under a bunch of small sticks or a pile of dust and then light them up. Each year, we hear that there will not be any on the market next year, but they always seem to turn up again around the first part of July. They can be a little dangerous, but nowadays it seems there is little fear of powder burns or the infections that they can cause.

When I was in knee pants and my brother Jack was a little older, Dad came home one Saturday night with some firecrackers, and of course we were not to touch them. When Dad got a chance, he told us, he would show us all about fireworks and how dangerous they were and how to shoot them off without hurting ourselves. But Grandpa lived with us there in Hickory Hollow, and being older and wiser, he took it upon himself to show us about firecrackers. "Come outside here boys and I'll show you about these things," he said.

Grandpa was not a big man, maybe five feet, six inches and about a hundred and thirty pounds. He walked with a steady gait and had a positive, but mischievous face. He had done a lot of hard work in his time and even then in his late sixties, for his size and age, he could out work anyone. He always smoked a pipe which he had a little trouble lighting. Grandpa had gotten his first false teeth when he was about forty years old, so they were getting nearly thirty years old and worn some. As he would draw through his pipe to light it, his upper teeth would drop loose and "clonk" against the pipe stem with each puff.

Grandpa, along with Jack and I, walked away from the house to the measured "clonk, clonk, clonk" of the pipe being lit. His pipe was full of tobacco and now burning pretty good. "Now, you see here boys, you gotta take 'em out of the package easy like," clonk, clonk, "so you won't tear the little string off. You want the fuse nice and long so they'll burn awhile and give you a chance to throw them. Now we don't need no matches. We'll just use my pipe." Clonk, clonk. Grandpa was still looking down at Jack and me as we stood there looking with open mouth anticipation. Grandpa puffed again and moved a real firecracker fuse closer to the burning tobacco. He looked out of the corner of his eye to see where he might toss the small explosive after he had it lit. At that instant, Jack and I heard and saw a big explosion right before our eyes. Somehow Grandpa had fumbled the firecracker too far into the burning tobacco, and BLEWEY! Pieces of the pipe zinged over our heads and burning tobacco ashes drifted to the ground like Roman candles.

It was pretty but didn't last long. Grandpa, of course, was just regaining his balance about three steps farther back. Only a short stem of pipe was clenched in his teeth. His nose was blackened and he fanned his fingers on his pant leg. They got a pretty good stinging. I think his pride was hurt more than anything, but the lesson on firecrackers was over. When he regained his composure, he said, "See there, boys, them !+&?$!# things is dangerous. Let that be a lesson to you."

It was.

This picture of Grandpa William O. French was taken when he was about 70 years old. He lived with us until he was in his nineties.

Grand Essentials

"The grand essentials to happiness in this life are something to do, something to love, and something to hope for." Joseph Addison

Uncle Elmo had big hands, skilled and full of purpose. Our family had gathered there at Elmo's place on the bottom road along with many other Frenches, all related one way or another to my dad. Elmo was Dad's brother and a few years younger than Dad. They worked together in the carpenter trade, building and repairing for the good folks along the Sangamon Bottoms, the third generation to do so.

Elmo was married to Zella. They had no children so everyone's children were special to them. Zella attended my birth, so she was one of the first to see me.

It may have been my grandmother's dinner or maybe Aunt Daisy's that brought so many of us together for big noontime spreads on summer Sundays. They were often referred to only as "Mom's dinner" (referring to Dad's and Uncle Elmo's mother, my grandmother Dena) or "Pop's dinner" to mark some birthday and needed no other identification. The men on that day were in dress pants and starched shirts, and being more comfortable in work clothes, they acted a little awkward in their dress-up clothes. In the shade of the Maple trees they talked of their work, of fishing, the weather and how good the crops looked in that fertile valley as they waited for the women to get all the dinner "fixens" just so.

During one break in the conversation, Uncle Elmo said, "I've got something in the garage I'd like to show you folks. I think we've got a little time." They all got up as men do, brushing grass and dust from their britches. The half-dozen men moved out toward Elmo's garage. I was no more than eight or nine years of age and only half as tall in stature as the others, but I followed along. One end of the garage was dug into the hillside to give some protection to Elmo's 1932 Chevy coupe. I could tell he was proud of the car by the way he rolled open the garage door. But it wasn't the car he wanted to show us. Elmo reached up to a cupboard, opened the door and slid out a box. He put the box on the work bench, and with his big hands he gently lifted out a small mechanical device. The machine had an upright can, a wheel, and piping. My eyes widened as I watched, standing there between those big men, spellbound as to what wonderful thing it might be. One of them said, "Well, I'll be! It's a toy steam engine." Elmo removed a small container from under the miniature boiler and added a spoonful of smelly, clear liquid. He slid it back under the boiler before measuring water into the upper part. Elmo then struck a match and touched it to the pan with the liquid. From my position with my chin just above the work bench, I could see a pretty blue flame playing around under the boiler can. I held my breath in wonder.

One asked, "How long will it take?"

"Oh, not long. Just a minute or two," Elmo answered in his easy voice. A tiny wisp of steam began to spray from a valve on the top. Bubbles formed at the end of the piping. Elmo gave the wheel a turn with his finger, and the little machine began a marvelous rhythm of turning the wheel and puffing out steam as a rod moved to and fro. I was amazed. I had never seen anything so interesting in all my life. Several grown men and a boy stood there in silence among the rich smells of oil, clay soil, and drying onions watching a tiny steam engine puff away.

The little engine ran along for several minutes before the blue flame began to play out, then it slowed. About that time, the women called out that it was time to eat dinner. Elmo, with his big gentle hands, put the fine little machine back upon the shelf in the cupboard. I wanted to see more of it. I would rather have watched it run than eat dinner, but that was not to be.

I thought of that engine a lot during the summer weeks that followed and knew I would like to have one for Christmas. As the summer ended and school began, as the leaves turned their colors and began to fall, as wood smoke from our stoves filled the hollow where we lived, I began to ask about getting a steam engine for Christmas. After several well-timed requests, my parents told me very strongly that there was not enough money to buy one child a toy so expensive. There were too many necessary things to buy and a toy steam engine was certainly not necessary. Besides that, there were my brothers and sisters to think about. So I felt a little ashamed but still the little steam engine filled my dreams.

We all grew older. War broke out in one place and then another till every side of the world seemed to be a battlefield. Elmo enlisted in the SeaBees, a branch of the Navy, saying that maybe if he went to war, someone with children like my dad or his brother, Dick, would not have to go. Elmo considered things like that.

He went away to Norfolk, Virginia, for training and came back home for awhile. Then he left Zella to tend to things as he went to the coast and sailed out under the Golden Gate Bridge on the USS Nordam on his way to New Guinea. Eventually, Elmo worked in the carpenters' shops of far off Milne Bay, making beautiful furniture out of native island woods for the military officers.

Aunt Zella wrote to him nearly every day about the goings-on along the Bottoms, about their cows, their sheep, and their hens. In the winter of 1942 she wrote of her quilting, of adding the pink patches now to the new one she was making. And later on she wrote about getting the garden made up in the spring. With family and friends helping occasionally, she endured alone there on those few acres.

The years passed, the war ended, and Elmo came home. Our own world began to take shape again. By then, the '32 Chevy had worn out and was sold for thirteen dollars, and a new '47 business coupe was in the hillside garage. I imagined the steam engine was still in the cupboard. I was now a fuzzy-faced kid. While helping Elmo on some chore I asked about the little steam engine. Could I see it run again? He said he no longer had it, that it was gone, given away to cousin Carl. For me, that was the end of the little steam engine, and I put it out of my mind.

I worked with Elmo later on in the family trade, watched him make precision fits in the wood he loved, using the tools he loved. I understood his appreciation for all things outdoors and his strict adherence to thrift.

Elmo was not all that old when he had a stroke. His condition grew worse, and he passed away. As I looked west toward a setting sun that day, I thought that there was now one less person on earth to enjoy this river valley.

Many seasons have passed and many suns have set in that valley since Elmo's passing. I talk of Elmo yet, of how he taught me to handle tools and work with wood, and I relate about the little steam engine in his garage that day beside the Chevy coupe. The thrill of seeing it as child never left me.

Some years later cousin Carl passed away. His wife Mary asked me to come to supper one night after his passing. We had a fine meal, and afterwards while visiting, she brought up the little steam engine. I was surprised she still had it. She said that Elmo had mentioned that I was always interested in it and had asked about it many times. He felt I should have it. She went to a closet and brought out the little steam engine and gave it to me. I had the same thrill on seeing it again as I had when I was a boy. It was a most treasured gift.

Some of Elmo's tools have been handed down to me, those tools that worked so well in his skilled hands. Some fifty-odd winters later, I sleep under the quilt that Zella wrote about in her letter of 1942, the quilt she added the pink patches to, and it keeps me warm. It is the Christmas season again, and it is these great gifts I now realize I have been given. They add to my happiness. I have something to do, I have something to love, and something to hope for.

Never Can Go Back They Say

In 1943 we moved out of Hickory Hollow and away from the hills and mud to a better place on the county road between Beardstown and Chandlerville. In a sense we had moved closer to civilization, toward what was called a better standard of living. We still used kerosene lamps for light, and Round Oak stoves for heating, but at this new place with a good house and fourteen acres, there were opportunities. Electric lines went by the property, and even a telephone was possible. Things were different here, a new world so to speak.

We kids changed schools. Grandpa was still with us, continuing to add another dimension to our lives, and Mom was able to get out and go to Home Bureau and Missionary meetings. Things were looking pretty good for us, and we all leaned into the task of bettering our lot in any way we could. Dad had to give up a large measure of his hunting and trapping, which was something he dearly loved to do. It was second nature to him. But with working ten hours a day doing carpenter work, and at the same time fixing up our new place, well, it didn't leave him, or anybody else, with much energy to spare.

Our Jersey cow continued to provide us with milk and an old sow gave us a mixed breed litter of pigs now and then. The pasture land was good and a few bales of hay for winter feed were easy enough to come by, but getting enough corn was a different story.

Some of the closest friends our family ever had were the Rawlings Family. Olin and Etta lived in the drainage district on college ground below Beardstown. In the fall they offered to let us pick up the corn left in the fields after the harvesting machines were through. Here was a chance for us to get some corn to feed our livestock through the winter without having to put out any money. So each Saturday and Sunday after church our whole family crowded into the '36 Chevy, drove down the road to Beardstown, went over the Sixth Street levy, and out the sand roads to Olin and Etta's place. It was our second home. They were always glad to see us, and even yet our family owes them so much.

We worked the weekends of October and were well into November and were feeling the damp chill of early winter. The Thanksgiving season was nearing and still we worked at the monotonous job of picking up corn. The shucks were always moist or wet. After picking and shucking out the first few ears, gloves and fingers became wet and stayed that way the rest of the day. The black gumbo soil stuck to my feet till they'd get so heavy I could hardly walk. I would give a fierce kick to shake it off, and maybe it would come off, but other times it wouldn't. The kick would throw me off balance till I'd fall to the ground with my half filled gunny sack of corn. These were long days for everybody, especially Dad as he watched the ducks flying from the river sloughs out to feed in the nearby fields. It was ideal duck hunting weather. A hunter's shot echoed up and down the river every now and then, adding to Dad's discomfort of picking up corn instead of hunting ducks.

We worked a couple of hours one Sunday morning and had come in for dinner at Etta's. She said that their Aunt Edith had come over earlier and invited everyone to her place to have an early Thanksgiving dinner. The turkey was especially big, and

Aunt Edith didn't want any left over. There was plenty to go around. They were people our family didn't know very well, but it sounded like a good idea to all concerned. And besides, never in all my twelve years had I ever tasted turkey. Dad always provided us with quail, pheasant and rabbit for Thanksgiving dinners. Now I was going to get the chance to eat that famous bird I had read about in my Elson-Gray reader. I had seen picture after picture of Pilgrims and Indians feasting with the great bird all baked up, brown and steaming in the middle of the table. I was delighted at the thought of a chance to see a real Thanksgiving table.

When we arrived, the men folk of Edith's family had already sat down around the table and were eating. I was so surprised to see the turkey had been all cut up. The meat had been sliced off the bone and someone already had a drumstick. Mom got plates for us kids, and began to fill them with some turkey, potatoes, carrots, and the like. I don't remember anyone giving thanks or saying a blessing. I sat down on stair steps in the front room with some other kids I didn't know and ate the tasteless white meat of my first Thanksgiving turkey. I really didn't see how anyone could tell it was turkey. I had never seen the Indians and Pilgrims doing this. I know I should have been thankful, but somehow I wasn't. I finished my plate and then sat on the floor as near to the stove as I could till it was time to go.

That evening, as we went bouncing toward home in the crowded, unheated Chevy, I wanted badly to be back in the warm little house in Hickory Hollow. Quail, rabbit, and pheasant were plenty good enough for Thanksgiving dinner, and a fire in the Heatrola was all I ever needed to warm me through and through.

I realized then and many times since that you never ever make it all the way back home…not even back to yesterday.

Eyeglasses

I made another trip over to the eye doctor to be checked for a change in glasses. I've gotten along pretty good, but the frames I've been wearing have never suited me like I wanted. They're okay if I'm sitting at a desk or for looking at myself in the mirror, but when it comes to bending over to sight a line or look under a log, they just won't stay put. The eye doctor mentioned they could be tightened to squeeze my head a little more so that they wouldn't move around.

I didn't like the idea much. I've already got dents in my head from the way I've been wearing them now. So I'm going back to the kind of glasses I started out with. They may be a little old fashioned, but they're by far the most practical for me, and besides, I've always thought more of gold than of plastic.

It seems a little out of tune in this day and age that we still must hang some wire and glass on our faces to see. Eyeglasses have been around some four-hundred years without a whole lot of change. Ben Franklin figured out the bifocal and that was quite a step forward. Now we have contacts, but I never thought much of sticking something in my eye. We can send humans to the moon and bring them back, but aside from cataract removal, we still have no secret formula or operation or medicine to restore vision. But I'm pleased my eyes are as good as they are, and all it takes is a lens in front to make them perfect.

Sight and the ability to see are surely miracles above all others. I cannot comprehend it. To a point, I can understand hearing. One wavering musical string can cause another string to move. A noisy truck going by can rattle a window. Far away thunder makes the light over the kitchen table jingle. The sound of one thing transferred to another. A thin piece of skin in my ear vibrates from some sound and I hear it. Easy enough to believe, but sight is another gift.

Almost every creature can see except the mole that for some reason was denied sight. Deer, I am told, don't see in color but in black and white, or maybe grey and white. We can see in color. Grass and leaves are green. At least, that's the color name we've given to them. Through these two smallest jewels in our head pass the pencil thin rays of light that get sorted out and transferred to images somewhere in our head. What a miracle. To me, it seems like the most complex part of our bodies.

I worked north of Peoria for a few years, and an old gentlemen named Tom came into the lumberyard the first of each month to cash his meager social security check. He'd bend over the counter with his nose not two inches from the check and his pencil point. He'd mark an "X". A very impressive mark in the way he made it. Tom was a proud old man living out his years with his sons by the river there. His eyes were as cloudy as an empty milk glass in the sink. But he often told me in our visits that his eyes were as good as any. He could see just as far as he needed to. In his southern way of speaking he'd say, "I can seed the stars at night and the moon. That's far enough for me." That was always final, and nobody questioned his eyesight.

Grandpa got his first eyeglasses soon after 1900 and was told not to be taking them off and on. "Just put 'em there and leave 'em."

That afternoon, Grandpa and my dad went up the east branch of the creek hunting for pheasant. In a short while, a dove fluttered an erratic course in front of them. Grandpa braced himself, pulled up his trusty shotgun, and emptied both barrels into the small bird. Dad yelled, "Here, here, Pop! What's the idea shooting a dove?" Grandpa pulled the new glasses down his nose and peered through the heavy smoke of the black powder shells and said, "By Gad! Looked big as a turkey buzzard through these spectacles."

He wore them in his pocket the rest of the hunt.

Of a Certain Persuasion

Mr. Schaad of Hickory Precinct, Sangamon Valley, would apologize to his horses. They shared a relationship that was close. He respected them, and his mare did likewise with him, it seemed.

Riding the cultivator and coming to the end of a row, Mr. Schaad would pull the reins to turn Kate and Star. Raising his voice, he'd say, "Kate! Kate! Come on around, come on around." Then with disappointment, he'd quickly say, "Oh! Oh! Sorry, Kate. Not you. I meant Star." Then with a gentler tone he would say, "Come on Star, on around, on around, that-a-girl, that-a-girl." And so the day went along with Mr. Schaad working his fields in kindly conversations with his horses.

In 1944 Ralph, our neighbor boy, was drafted off the farm to fight in the war. His first letters home were hard for him to write and difficult for his folks to read. He was doing okay, getting to meet new people and making friends in the ranks, but there was much between the lines they couldn't figure out. They found no depth in his words.

Weeks passed; Ralph wrote again in a more relaxed script. He asked about the cows, called them by name, asked if the new calf had come yet. What was it like? Was there plenty of hay and grain to see them through till the spring pastures greened up?

With that letter, Ralph the soldier was writing with interest and enthusiasm. The words and questions came from the son as they knew him to be. He was away from home and missed the cows. His folks were reassured that Ralph was just fine and had not forgotten where he came from.

My brother Jack was drafted into the army when I was a junior in high school. He had done the milking of our Jersey cow up to that time. Now it was my responsibility. The smell of the barn lot, the hay in the loft, the straw bedding and the early morning exercise made for a pleasant experience.

It wasn't long before the cow and I had a comfortable routine. I gave her two flakes of alfalfa hay and six ears of corn chopped into the feed box. She began her breakfast as I sat on the three-legged stool, eased my head against her soft belly and began the rhythm that guided fresh streams of milk into the pail.

One especially cold December morning, a strong northwest wind blew across two icy rivers, countless sloughs, streams, and ten thousand acres of frozen ground before whistling through the cracks in our hillside barn. I shivered as I threw down that hay. I shivered as I chopped the ears of corn. I sat down on the milking stool and leaned my head against the cow and noticed she was shivering, too. Her large muscles quaked and shook in the cold, drafty barn.

I finished the milking and wondered what I could do about the shivering cow. I had a warm house to go to, but what about the cow? I put down an extra flake of hay, then added more straw bedding to the north side of the barn. I stood there awhile feeling empathy for the cow.

By now there was morning light. In a few minutes I began my walk east, then turned south up the Houck Hill road and continued on for two more miles till I came to the Bierhaus corner where I met the school bus. But I worried about the cow. She was on my mind all day. I learned how close I had become to her.

When I was fifteen years old, I bought two ewes for twenty-five dollars "with my own money," as they say. Dad didn't much want any sheep on the place. Yet when the pasture began to look like a park and the brush more controlled, he softened his opposition.

I would be out in the pasture cutting thistles or picking blackberries or some such chore and the ewes would be far off, a hundred yards or more. Without me noticing, they would come near. I would hear them munching the grass, and then they would sniff my shoes. They would lean their soft, thick wool against my leg. I could smell their rich lanolin. They were good company, and I liked being in their presence. I liked their gentle ways and the lambs they gave me each spring.

The draft board sent me a greeting, too. At five o'clock on a crisp May morning, Dad drove me down to Beardstown where I boarded a bus with two dozen other sad-faced boys. We were off to the military during the Korean conflict. Yes, I missed the sheep, missed my lambs. They were as much my family as any of the others, and I missed them all.

When I returned a few years later, Dad had thirty-two sheep in the pasture with not a single weed in sight. He must have comes to terms with having sheep on the place. My joy had multiplied. Dad was a good shepherd and proud of his flock.

During the Christmas season, I see the Nativity scenes with Joseph and Mary and the newborn baby. Standing close by are the cow, the donkey, and always a few sheep. I wonder how Joseph felt about his animals. Why did he bring them on the long journey? Didn't he have enough on his mind with Mary about to deliver at any time? Childbirth in that day and age would have been risky business. Joseph worried. He was under stress.

I think he wanted his animals along for his own comfort and support. I believe he was a man of a certain persuasion. I can imagine him with an arm over the donkey's shoulder while talking softly to him, as Mr. Schaad would have done. Joseph would have missed his own cow if he had left her behind, just as Ralph missed his cows and worried over their comfort, just as I worried over the comfort of ours in the drafty barn.

The sheep were no bother and furnished a calm contentment throughout the night. This gathering by the stable was all about extending kindnesses to each other and caring for something or someone other than themselves. Isn't that what Christmas is all about?

It's a comforting thought for me.

Where Angels Play

Hickory Road wanders north and west out of the county seat town of Virginia. It follows the overland stage road for some distance. About five miles out, it drops into a deep hollow and soon crosses Schaad Creek where there was once a wooden bridge. The road curves soon after and begins a steep climb up and over Ainsworth Hill. From the top of the hill is a beautiful view of all the streams, hollows, and sculptured hills. Grazing cows and Cedar trees dot the landscape. A broad crescent of the Sangamon Valley lies to the north, the east and the west for miles and miles.

In the olden days, the road was reasonably good out to about the bridge. From there on, it was difficult to maintain. In winter and spring, it was nearly impassable, even for horse and wagon. In the late thirties, the township commissioners proposed that a new route be found so the hill would not be such an obstruction to year-round traffic.

A surveying team arrived in late November after the leaves had fallen. Brooks Bender, a civil engineer and land surveyor, was assigned the task. Cordelia, often called Code, was his rod man. They spent the better part of a month studying, sighting the elevations, and driving grade stakes along Hickory Hollow and Schaad Creek.

One day as they were ending up their work, Bender said to Code, "Have you noticed anything unusual in the way these trees grow?"

"I don't understand what you're asking," replied Code.

"Come here. Take a sight through this."

Code laid his rod against a shrub and leaned forward, putting his eye to the high powered glass. In the magnified view, nothing was unusual to him. Just hundreds of Cedar trees scattered over the slopes and creek banks. "Sure are a lot of Cedar trees," he said as he straightened and looked around.

"Look again," said Bender. "Notice how uniform they are? Looks as though they've been trimmed and shaped. Very unlikely out here in the wild. Trunks are smooth and round, crowns are perfect cones. Cedar trees don't grow that way."

"It doesn't bother me a bit how trees grow," Code replied as he lifted his rod and started for the warmth of the truck some distance away. The winter sky was cloudy, calm, and gray. High overhead were the muted sounds of ducks and geese in their migratory conversations.

As Bender stood alone among the small trees, bits of sleet began to fall. It came in a mystic, audible hush with each natural element reflecting its own sound. Every cedar had a whispering voice, the shrubs yet another. The dry leaves and grass spoke, too.

Bender relaxed and felt the warmth and comfort of his own soft clothing. He moved to touch a Cedar tree, then to touch another. His vision could see no man-made thing. He felt ageless, neither young nor old. There was no indication of the time in which he lived. It could have been a thousand years before or in some future time. A mild euphoria came over him. Some would say he was hearing the angels sing. By all this, he knew there was something significant about the cedars and the place where he stood.

Bender was reluctant to leave, but darkness was closing in. He turned, removed the transit from the tripod, brushed off bits of ice and nested it into the padded wooden box. He folded the tripod, laid it over his shoulder and began his walk to join Code.

The next day was messy underfoot with the melting of sleet and light snow that followed it. So the surveyors did not leave Virginia. It would be a restful day, void of walking any hills. But the pleasant interlude among the cedars was still on Bender's mind.

He stopped at Campbell's Barber shop on the southwest corner of the square for a little company and a haircut. While he waited, he overheard old timers tell of the abundance of game and good hunting in the early days along the Sangamon bottoms.

He listened awhile. When he felt he could, he asked if any of them had noticed the Cedar trees growing in that area, so many of them so perfectly shaped.

"You mean out around Hickory and the Ainsworth Hill?" they asked.

"That's the place," he answered.

The loafers began talking over each other's voices, assuring him there was a story about the place. They couldn't tell it. It was Walt, napping in a chair by the stove, who knew about it. "Lived out that way," they explained.

In a raised voice, one called out, "Walter, wake up! Man here wants to know about them Cedar trees out along the bottom near Hickory."

Walt straightened in his chair, passed a hand over his face and asked, "What's this about the trees?"

Bender explained his work and about seeing so many finely shaped Cedar trees. He figured there must be some explanation.

"Well," Walt began, "those trees puzzle a lot of people. I know a little of how they came about. They were first noticed forty or so years ago. Seems there was a man—a hunter, trapper and carpenter—that lived near there. His name was Mory. The house in the hollow where he lived has mostly fallen in now. Had a big family, both boys and girls. Lived there by the creek and provided for them as best he could, which was pretty good at that."

Walt continued, "In early December one year, the youngest girl took sick. She was six or seven years old. Believe Ashlee was her name. It was a very serious condition in those days and didn't look good for her. The child was in a hospital some thirty miles away. The wife stayed with her day and night. So Mory had his mother, Melissa, come to help out. That way, the kids could stay in school and Mory could tend to his traps and keep a little money coming in. Times was tough, as any of us here can tell you. Especially hard on Mory. The family had never been apart and he wanted them all back together again. He hoped Ashlee could be well and home by Christmas. But I'm getting a little ahead of my story here," Walt said. "Those Cedar trees you're talking about—around here they was always called Christmas trees. Didn't know 'em by any other name. Called 'em that winter and summer.

"Anyway, Mory would watch for the best Christmas tree along his trap line. He'd see one and always thought he could make it more perfect. With his Bartlow knife, he'd nip off a branch here and there. It almost became an obsession with him. Couldn't pass up a Cedar tree without a little trimming. That winter with his daughter sick, the best he could find was going to be Ashlee's Christmas tree.

"Mory's last trip to the hospital had left him especially saddened. The infection was draining the life from little Ashlee.

Mory had not always been a very religious man, but he had married a good woman whose father was a tent preacher. So by now, his wife was bringing him a little closer to knowing the Lord. Mory saw the Lord in the beauty of nature, and every day he spent among the fields and streams was for him an ongoing communion. During Ashlee's illness, Mory learned to pray. Told me that himself," Walt emphasized. "By then, it was past the middle of December, just about this time of year. Winter had set in pretty hard. From here on, the story almost tells itself.

"Late in the day, Mory was returning home along a cow path around Ainsworth Hill. He was feeling tired on tired and carrying with him the disgrace of a fifty cent possum and the toes of a mink for all his trapping efforts. He was cold. His despair was almost complete and hope was thin. Ahead of him on the uphill side was a small cedar. It called to him and his Barlow knife. He approached it to trim a branch and thought this might be the tree for Ashlee. At the thought of her, he was overcome with emotion. He fell to the ground at the base of the tree and sobbed away his burdens. A prayer rose up out of him, and he prayed hard and strong to the only Lord he knew. 'Please, Lord of these hills and streams,' he said, 'Please, Lord of this valley, if you have the power and it is your wish, take the sickness from my daughter. Bring her home. Bring her home for Christmas. I'll be your servant as best I can to the very end, if only my Ashlee can be well again,' he prayed.

"Mory lay awhile on the deep natural carpet of winter grasses and smelled the essence of the earth, looked up to the darkening sky and heard the migrating birds. He regained his composure and felt much relieved with just a tinge of guilt for bargaining with the Lord. But that would have to stand. The tiredness left Mory. He was warm again. He stood, gathered the cedar in his hands, pulled it toward him and breathed in the fragrance. He turned and walked on home. He entered the warm house and a waiting supper with his mother and all the other children. Melissa said to him, 'There was no mail today, but Mister Treadway came to the door to tell me people in town was saying little Ashlee was some better today.' Under his breath, Mory gave thanks. In his heart, he felt something had changed. In his mind, he saw Ashlee and all the family around the Christmas tree in the front room of the house.

"A few days before Christmas, Ashlee did come home. As soon as she was able, Mory bundled her up and carried her on his back to the Cedar tree where he had prayed. Ashlee sat on the thick grass beside the cow path while Mory, with his trusty knife, cut away at the small trunk of their Christmas tree. They were a happy pair as they went toward home with Ashlee carrying the tree while Mory carried Ashlee. From that day on, he never trimmed another Cedar tree. Nor did he have to. It just seemed that by some blessing, all the cedars growing there took on the nicest shapes and it continues to this day. But I guess you already know that." Walt concluded.

Bender grinned broadly, thanking Walter for relating the story, knowing that he himself could hardly wait to return to the rural hillside. He knew the place where angels played and prayers and Cedar trees were one and the same.

The Last Christmas Cards

Annie was a small woman, some would even say slight. Yet she was more than adequate in a mother's determination to care for her family and run a proper household. She was clean, neat, and smart and had some style about her. However, Annie deserved a better situation.

She had married well enough, but the stress of running a home and raising three boys on her husband's limited income and endless empty promises was taking its toll. They had reduced the heat to save a few bucks but there were times when she just wanted to be warm, at least for a little while.

Andy was not lazy. He had a steady job. The problem was that he just couldn't get home with all he was paid. He meant well, but something in a man makes him want to be the hero, to strut into the house and hand his woman more than enough dollars, more than just the bacon. He wants to present the whole hog. Andy wanted very much to do that. He knew he could if only the cards would fall his way. It became an obsession with him. Unfortunately, his card playing buddies were more skilled than he was. Part of Andy's paycheck was diluted in the dim and smoky card rooms and ended up going home in other men's pockets. He ached at his failures, making promises to himself every time never to get caught up in a card game again.

Winter was nudging in. Rain had come and then frozen, followed by sleet and on that day, a dusting of snow, all reminders that weeks and weeks of winter with the extra expenses were just ahead.

Annie was angry and distressed at the shortage of cash. She prayed for an improvement in the situation as she put the supper on the table and all sat down. After finishing dinner and when the boys had gone to do their own things, Annie said to Andy, "There has to be a change here. We can't go on this way. Our expenses are mounting. Christmas is coming and we don't have a spare dime. Those boys deserve a decent Christmas. Please stay away from the cards."

Andy agreed, leaned back in his chair and said, "Don't worry your pretty little head. In a couple of weeks, I'll be getting my Christmas bonus. We'll be on Easy Street. You can go to the IGA and fill a grocery cart, maybe two. Get whatever you want for the boys. And I want you to spend some money on yourself, too. Get your hair done. Buy some shoes, new pajamas. You wait and see. We'll have a dandy Christmas." Although she had heard it before, like a good wife, Annie wanted to believe it.

Their small tree was decorated with strings of popcorn, paper chains and cranberries. Red and green cellophane wreaths hung in the windows. There was a coziness in the small house. The winter days passed. Soon it was late in the week just before Christmas. Darkness came early. A cold, blustery wind made the tree limbs rattle and street lights sway. Eerie shadows moved on the frosted glass. The furnace murmured and rumbled, driving cold from the room to add a measure of comfort.

Annie was growing tense. "Andy should be home by now with the bonus money," she thought. She had been thinking about it all day, hoping against hope that he would do as promised and come straight home with all the money.

Annie told the boys she had an errand to run but they should help themselves to the soup she had prepared for supper. She put on a long coat over her apron, a scarf on her head, and thrust her hands deep down in her pockets as she went out.

Most of the shops were closed and dark. Only a few cars could be seen. Annie went down the south alley, looking for what she did not want to find—Andy's car and a broken promise. She searched with uneasy steps. The rough ice and cold went through the thin soles of her shoes. No one else moved about. Annie was alone.

She crossed Main Street, turned north up the east alley past the old livery stable, past the rear of an empty hotel, past trash cans and barking dogs. A dim light shone through the rear window of the pool hall. The sound of men's voices distilled out into the night. A few paces further was Andy's car. Frost covered the surfaces, proving to Annie that it had been there for some time.

Anger and disappointment began to rise up in her. Her slim body quaked from the cold and anxiety. With halting steps and light breathing, she approached the pool hall door. Looking through the dirty glass past a window shade, she saw a circle of men sitting like monks in meditation, each with a hand of cards. Andy was there with no joy on his face. There was a pile of money on the table. "Andy's bonus money," she thought. The sight was too much for her.

With the strength that only women know about, coming from some other source, she turned the knob and gave the door a mighty kick. It flew open like a clap of thunder. The men froze, wondering what was coming next. For a brief moment, there was a terrible silence like a burning fuse.

Annie looked around, spotting the only weapon she knew—a strong-handled broom. She grabbed it and put every ounce of her strength into a magnificent swing. Broom straw, hats, playing cards and green back dollars scattered in every direction. Big men showed fear. She swung again and again and again till there was not a straw left in the broom or a man left in the room, save for Andy cowering, petrified and disheveled in a darkened corner.

Annie gave him a withering look of disgust and then looked at all the money. Sobbing quietly in the now still room, without hurrying, she began picking up the bills, ironing them with her hand, turning each one so all the denominations were upright and neatly in place.

When no more could be found, she stood up, dried her eyes, and put the money in an apron pocket. She closed her coat over the winnings and stepped out into the night. The sky was crisp and clear. The stars were bright and beautiful. She saw in them the promise of a new direction with no more cards. "Thank you, Lord," she whispered.

***

There was honor among the circle of card players present on the cold winter night when Annie emptied the room. None of them ever claimed or asked for any of the money. It was a long, long time before they even talked about it. Andy played no more cards.

In the spring, Annie and her family did find a new direction. They moved closer to Andy's work and farther from the influences that played on his weaknesses.

The boys adjusted to the new location and actually thrived on it. By fall, they were ready to march off to a new school where education and social opportunities were greater than the ones left behind.

A few years later, I was shopping in a department store near where they had moved. As I passed the women's department,

I noticed a clerk who looked familiar. With a bit of recall, I realized it was Annie. "Unbelievable!" I thought. Frown lines and stress lines were gone. Her hair was beautiful.

Annie was no longer thin but rounded out till curves and contours made her a striking model. She moved with the confidence of a happy lady.

I felt immense admiration for her, felt good that she had the strength and determination to get where she wanted to be. She deserved no less.

The Drifting Ball Pitcher

There is a lot of interest in ball games in our area now with softball, slo-pitch, and women's teams all around. It seems a good summertime sport and some of the teams get pretty good.

There was a lot of interest around here in the early 1920's too. The rivalry between the towns in the county was pretty strong, as it is now. Virginia didn't mind being beaten so much by Chandlerville, Ashland, or some other town, but they sure didn't like to lose to Beardstown boys. However, they often did.

A lot of construction work was going on in and around Virginia at the time with various hard roads being built, the oil pipeline going through, and many lineman gangs putting in electrical or telephone and telegraph cables everywhere. Many people followed these crews as workers, but there were always some drifters passing through in their company, either waiting for work or just out of work. One such fellow took up residence at the Mann Hotel for a period of time.

Among the visiting and gossiping that went on around the shady loafing benches, it came out that this fellow had been a pretty good pitcher for a big ball club. The word was passed around till a Mr. Finn heard about it. Now Mr. Finn sponsored a ball team and had a strong desire to win an upcoming game with Beardstown. He approached the middle-aged gentleman as he sat on a bench in front of the hotel. Finn looked him over for quite awhile, then walked to the corner, looked back, and studied him some more. He jiggled some change in his pocket, then walked over and stood beside the could-be pitcher in the morning shade.

"Boy, boy," he said, "I hear you used to play some ball. Any truth to that, boy?"

The man looked at Mr. Finn for a long moment through bloodshot eyes. Then he spat and answered slowly, "Used to play some ball. Yes I did."

"Can you pitch a good ball?" was the next question.

"I used ta could," he answered.

Mr. Finn handed the drifter five dollars and told him to come out to the ball park that evening behind the C. P. and St. L. depot. "Show us what you can do, boy. Okay?" asked Mr. Finn.

Well, Mr. Finn had made the mistake of paying the man ahead of time for in a few hours the old ball player was well nigh to numb at a local saloon. Mr. Finn found him and walked him and stayed right with him the rest of the day and into the evening. Next morning, he took him out to the diamond himself. It was a hot summer day and the playing field was dry and dusty from the previous evening's game. The sun was up good and surely the old drifter's head was pounding hard, but Mr. Finn wanted to know if he had a ball player, a real pitcher, or not. He took the mound in beads of sweat, three day's growth of beard, and an unsteady stance. The diamond was vacant except for the two men. Mr. Finn was dressed in a Stetson, a fine grey suit with a gold chain and watch across his vest, and highly polished shoes. The dapper fellow took a bat and went to the batter's position, tapped the ground a couple of times, then held the bat straight out. "Now, boy, boy. Can ya, now boy? Can you hit my bat?"

Mr. Finn was tense. The man on the mound pitched the ball up in the air a couple of times and hesitated. Then pitched it up again. The bat waited. He drew a breath, spun and threw a ball straight as an arrow that ticked the bat and exploded against the old wooden backstop. "That a way, boy. Now do it again."

The pitcher burned another one right on target. Ka Pow! And another and another. His eyes were wider now, and he was chewing his cud of tobacco at a faster rate. He took a few fingers of dust, threw the ball in the air, and ran a little jog around the pitcher's mound. Mr. Finn was ecstatic. He threw the bat and let out another yell only to be answered by a yell from the pitcher who had come to life again. Mr. Finn danced his shiny shoes around in the dust and right out to the pitcher's mound. He pulled fifty dollars out of his wallet and showed it to the born again ball player. He reached for it as Mr. Finn drew it back. "Now, now, wait a minute, boy. Take it easy," Finn said. "We got a big game coming up Saturday at Beardstown, see. We want to win it bad. You stay and pitch that game for us Saturday and, win or lose, the fifty dollars is yours. Okay, boy?" A deal was struck.

Mr. Finn stayed pretty close to his new pitcher, hardly letting him out of his sight and saw some of the best pitching around Virginia that he'd seen in a long time. The pitcher was only being charitable if he threw a ball that anybody could hit.

Saturday came and the ball team and Mr. Finn had a real pride about them, a lot of confidence in their new teammate. He was still sober and in good spirits, clean shaven, good looking ball suit, but still chewing a cud of tobacco. He arrived in Beardstown. A convoy of fans and well-wishers in Model T Fords, Whippits, Star cars, a Buick or two, and a few surreys followed.

There was the usual warm-up, and then the game began. Mr. Finn stood by jingling some coins in his pocket of his tailored suit. The Beardstown team had a lot of assurance at the beginning of the game, but it began to fade as Virginia's new hot-shot pitcher struck them out, one by one. He let them hit an occasional ball to make the game interesting. Virginia won, hands down. It was a tremendous victory for Virginia and the fans were wild with excitement.

After the game, Mr. Finn patted the pitcher on the back and said, "Now boy, boy. That was a real game. Some beautiful pitching there that was. Here's your fifty dollars just like I said. Now boy, we got a game this Thursday at Arenzville. What do you say, will you come with us?"

The gentlemen took the fifty dollars and walked on through the crowd without answering. That was the last anybody really knew of him. Some say he was around Beardstown for while. He spent some time at the Sazarac and slept down by the levee. Then nobody seems to know where he went, but one thing positive, he sure gave Mr. Finn and Virginia a good day at the ball game.

Thatcher's Barn

I have worked on many barns in my years of carpentry with my dad, my uncle, and my brothers. We roofed them, painted them, shored up their lofts, and repaired the cupolas. I have never worked in a barn but what I didn't find a personal place with some measure of comfort, a place where there was a seat or a chair by a feed box or some such spot. There would be pencil marks on old pine boards, of bushels of grain, bales of hay, of cows and sows being bred and birthed. Rainy days were spent there in contemplation or worry. Always there was a comforting sound of the farm animals. This was the farmer's own space, a personal place.

Thatcher had spent many odd years on that section of land split by Schaad Creek in Hickory Precinct. He worked the timber with a big bay horse and plowed and planted the fields and bottom lands to crops in their own season. It was a good life, not one of easy wealth, but never through the years was there ever much to want for.

Thatcher had come in early at the urging of his wife. "It's a holiday, you know. You don't have to work all the time. Especially Christmas," she said. But a holiday and idleness can weigh heavy on a man more comfortable in work. Anyway, he rested and watched out the windows, watched the sky, the fallow fields.

Toward evening he was feeling the same restlessness he felt every eve before Christmas. It was almost a calling, an unfinished bit of activity he felt a need to do. But he put it aside and watched across the fields again.

Thatcher's wife had been in the kitchen all day. The house smelled good of baking bread, of pies, brown sugar and molasses. Thatcher and his wife and daughters gathered around a big kitchen table for a sumptuous meal of blessedness and plenty that had been raised by their own hands in the good earth around them. By the time they finished, the sun lay low and finally made its descent into the hills. They felt the winter chill and saw the darkness come. Thatcher sat in his rocker and read for awhile, but he still had something yet to do. He got out of his chair and called to his oldest daughter, "April, would you help me in the barn a little while tonight?"

His wife quickly replied, "Now, Thatcher. She's got things to do in here, and a barn is no place for a girl."

"Well, I think it is tonight," he replied. April was anxious to go.

So after putting on their coats and overshoes, Thatcher and his daughter left the warmth of the house and trudged across the yard and barn lot by lantern light. "Look at the night sky, April. You can see stars in only half the sky. Bet we have some weather coming in. Might be snow." They passed the pens and heard the low tones of old geese in their own conversations. The animals in the barn—the bay horse, the Jersey cow, the sheep in the lean-to—recognized their coming. In the silence of the night, one could hear their resting sounds, each one to its own kind. They were good and comfortable sounds.

Thatcher opened the door and hung the lantern on a high hook, safe away from all straw and hay. It cast a golden glow over the mellow wood of feed boxes, barn beams, and mangers.

It shone on the face of the cow, the head and mane of the horse. The blue cat joined them, taking her rightful place on a box where she'd had her kittens.

Thatcher asked April to climb the ladder to the loft. "When you get up there, find the brightest straw," he said. "Throw several armfuls down to the hallway."

April was a good climber and in a minute was in the loft. As soon as her eyes adjusted to the darkness, she found the brightest straw and threw a great pile of it down to her father. She joined him then, and scattered the straw deeply on the earthen floor of the horse's stall. They filled the mangers too, and put plenty around the Jersey cow.

"Notice how each kind of animal has its own smell, April? The horse rich of salt and sweat and leather, the cow of sweetness, and the sheep, the richness of wool."

"I think they're good smells," said April.

"I do too," said Thatcher. "Healthy and contented animals always smell that way."

Together father and daughter spread the bedding straw throughout the small barn. April finally asked, "Dad, why are we cleaning up the barn and spreading all this straw on Christmas Eve?"

Thatcher leaned on his pitchfork and said, "I think a barn is a special place. Women have their kitchens. Men have their barns. Much comes to life in a barn. A barn sees a lot of birthing. Remember all the lambs last March, and the wobbly legged calf? Remember the colt? And the old blue cat there always chooses to have her kittens here in the barn."

"Yeah. I know," said April. "but nothing's going to be born out here tonight."

"Maybe not," Thatcher said, "but remember the story of long, long ago about a baby being born in a manger?"

"You mean the baby Jesus?"

"That's the one."

"But Dad! This is just a little old barn."

"I know, April, but I don't remember that barn in Bethlehem being very big."

"Gee, just think," she said, "that little baby was surrounded by fresh straw and the same animals we have here."

"You betcha. Same gentle smell, too. There's something about a barn that makes birthing less scary. I believe old Joseph in the story knew what he was doing. It's no mystery to me why he took Mary to a stable barn after her long ride on that bony donkey. I'll bet he knew they were in for a pretty restless night, and he preferred the familiar comforts of the barn. There was a baby born, you know. Changed the world, too." Thatcher stood silent so all was quiet.

He looked at his daughter and said, "You know, it happened once. It could happen again and maybe right here." At that, they both grinned widely, their eyes sparkling. Their work was done. The barn was ready, just in case.

Thatcher took the lantern off the hook, then stood still and listened intently before he whispered, "I think it's snowing."

"How do you know?" she whispered back.

He pointed a finger upward and said, I can hear it on the roof." They both laughed at that and walked out of the barn.

It surprised April to see that it really was snowing. Enough was on the ground to make their lantern much brighter. Walking arm in arm through the sparkling snow, they made their way back to the warm comforts of the house. Now April knew why her father had always spent time in the barn on the night before Christmas. That night he shared the reason with her. It was a small miracle of another kind.

HICKORY ROAD

Every Christmas during the 1940's, this small barn in Hickory Precinct waited for a miracle. The lot fences and the lean-to that sheltered the sheep had long since rotted away when this picture was taken about 1974. Now even the barn is gone, but the earth where it stood remains rich in the smell of hay and grain and farm animals.

I went there looking for cedar boughs and I heard the low tones of old geese and farm animals in their resting, the purring of the blue cat. I stood for awhile and listened.

The Radio

I have a small, battery operated radio. I move it from my bedside to the breakfast table. The batteries that run it are small, maybe the size of my finger, and it runs quite awhile on one of those finger-sized batteries.

It's a whole lot different than the table radio that Dad brought home from Rexroat Brothers Store sometime back in the thirties. Besides the radio, he carried in a large black and white striped Burggess battery. It was the size of a big loaf of bread and twenty times heavier. We also had to string up an insulated antenna wire from the house to the Mulberry tree by the creek. It was quite a thrill when we got it hooked together and the right wires plugged into the striped battery.

Our little house in the hollow was filled with all kinds of new sounds and events. The radio was a frail connection to a nearly unknown world that reached on past the ends of our muddy roads. The thin wire antenna sifted the heavy air of that hollow and picked out the voices of Winston Churchill, President Roosevelt, Julian Bentley, and Gabriel Heater. On Saturday night, if the battery was strong and the air just right, we could hear the WLS barn dance from Chicago or the Grand Ole Opry from some far away place called Nashville. The radio was a marvel that none of us understood but only enjoyed. On other nights we heard Bob Hope, Jack Benny, Amos and Andy, or laughed along with Fibber McGee and Molly and heard Johnny "Call for Phillip Mor...ree...iss."

Jack and I got up on week day mornings, dressed, ate our oatmeal, and listened to Jolly Joe before school. Later in the day we hurried over Hickory Hill toward home to hear a few minutes of Jack Armstrong, the All-American Boy. That radio sharpened our imaginations more than anything I know of. We imagined what the Lone Ranger looked like. In our minds we saw the horse and fought the battles.

All those voices and programs fade in and out of my memory, but the importance of a Joe Louis fight in about 1939 was surely the greatest thing. But it seemed the big black and white battery was always weak on those fight nights. Probably the station was so far away that it was difficult to pick up the signal.

Boxing on the radio was Dad's greatest listening pleasure, and he could spread the thrill and excitement to the rest of us. His enthusiasm was contagious. The radio was left off as much as possible all day so as not to waste the battery. When fight time came in the evening, Dad pulled his rocker up as close as he could to the radio. We kids sat on a stool or bench close by. Mom did whatever had to be done very quietly. The kerosene lamp cast shadows on the wall and the Heatrola stove behind us warmed the room.

"Be still now, boys," Dad said as he turned the knob. Click! A fuzzy little light came on behind the dial and the radio buzzed and hummed. In a few moments we heard scratchy voices. They got stronger. "From Madison Square Garden in New York City. . . .The Gillette Safety Razor Company brings you the heavyweight boxing champions of the world. Tonight with ten knockouts and no losses, Joe. . . . Lewis."

The crowd went wild with cheers and applause. Dad with his imagination was right there in the ring, and his sons weren't far behind. The radio station faded away but we could hear the bell strike and round. The station came back in strong. We heard the punching and the announcer calling the punches. Dad's rocking chair squeaked with each hit. He twitched and tightened his arms as punches were called out. "Louis, an uppercut to the jaw, a hard right to the shoulder. He takes a punch on the side. Man, oh man! This is a fight tonight."

The crowd cheered wildly and the station faded away. As it did, our heads moved in closer. But there was no sound. Dad muttered something. I asked, "Where is Madison Square Garden?"

He said, "Hush up, quiet," as he strained his every fiber, trying to hear a whisper. Finally he reached up and turned the radio off and said, "We'll rest the battery a little while."

We all relaxed some and leaned back. In a minute or so, Dad reached for the knob and all our heads bumped in front of the speaker. When the radio came on, it was the fourth round and Joe Lewis was punching away. The Gillette Safety Razor was giving more smooth shaves than any other kind. Then the reception faded fast and I don't remember how the fight ended, but Joe Louis remained the heavyweight champion of the world. We had heroes then.

I'm sure there were other great moments on that table radio for many Burggess batteries were used and discarded to the creek over the years. But never were the moments greater, never were our imaginations fired so much as on fight night with a weak battery.

Season of Hope

Christmas can be a time of mixed feelings, a time when emotions play around inside you, never telling for sure whether it's happiness or otherwise. Sometimes those feelings come out as a smiling lump in your throat.

I was riding east on a Rock Island train coming out of the mountains, heading home for Christmas. At Calhan, Colorado, we came to an abrupt stop with the remains of an old Chevy wrapped around the front of the diesel engine.

The lady driving the car was rushing to town with several crates of eggs in the back seat. They would soon have been traded for cash, a little Christmas money. But nothing survived, neither her nor any of the eggs. So my feelings of gladness for going home at Christmas were tempered with sadness for an unknown lady making a final dash to town, hoping for Christmas money in her purse.

Later we met the Denver Rocket at Limon and took on more passengers. Down the aisle came a lady, maybe ten years older than I. She had honey blond hair and a plain face without expression. She was dressed neatly but in ordinary fashion. Her eyes met no one else's. She sat down against the window across from me and folded her hands on a small travel case in her lap. I sat at my window across the aisle with no one between us.

The plains of eastern Colorado slipped by, an endless monotony of snowy landscape broken occasionally by a jack rabbit or antelope racing the sharp prairie wind.

Hours passed. The lady's expression remained unchanged. I watched her reflected face as she stared out the window at the nothingness.

I got up, stood in the aisle and said, "Excuse me. Would you like some company?"

Somewhat startled, she looked up. Her eyes were moist, but she nodded approval toward the empty seat beside her. She pulled her cloth coat closer around her.

Many miles went by before either of us spoke. Finally I asked, "Going home for Christmas?" She drew a sigh and said yes.

"To Chicago?" I questioned.

"No, Newton, Iowa," she replied.

"Taking some vacation time?" I continued.

"No, no. This is something I just had to do. Had to have a few days."

I absorbed her mixed feelings and words for what they were worth. She seemed hesitant to talk, yet not rejecting. "Do you have family in Newton?" I asked.

She looked down and ran a thumbnail around the seam of her travel bag. Then she started slowly, more positive. "Yes. My mother is there. She has my two girls." Her face became much more expressive. Her eyes quickened. "I miss them so much." she said. "You see, my husband left about a year ago. I don't know where he went, but I imagine California. He has people there. Money was scarce, so my two girls and I moved in with Mom. Then finally, I had to go to Denver to find work. That was in April, and I haven't seen any of them since."

She talked easily now. Her hands were busy making expressions or pulling at her gloves. The swaying car kept an easy rhythm with the singing rails beneath us. The yellow glow of farmhouse windows measured our coming and going. The young woman talked on as the miles passed by, emptying out, unloading everything that was pulling her down. She thought that maybe somewhere out there, her husband was on his way to Iowa, too. "I don't know what makes me think that," she said. "I have no reason to think so. But there is a chance he might be. I hope so. I do hope so. Even if just for the day."

Such a different person she was now. Radiant, alive, not at all like the girl that had boarded at Limon. We passed the lights and warmth of Lincoln, across the frozen Platte and wide Missouri and on into Omaha, heading for Newton on the Rock Island line. The girl, now with visions of a homecoming, relaxed down into her seat and drifted off to sleep.

I returned to my seat and covered up with my woolen army coat. Later in the night, I felt a hand on my shoulder. I came awake to see the golden-haired girl smiling down at me, a Christmas angel in the half-light of the passenger car.

"Sorry to wake you," she said softly. "But I'll be getting off soon. I couldn't leave without saying thank you for getting me to talk, for letting me talk the way I did. Thank you." Weary eyed and amused, I nodded my acceptance.

She made her way to the end of the car and then looked back before going out the door. She was smiling, happy for the moment, filled with hope even when there was little reason to be hopeful.

I never saw her again, of course, so I have no way of knowing how her story ended that Christmas. But I've remembered her many times over the years and thought if Christmas is anything at all, it is the season of hope...even the slimmest kind.

Winter Doldrums and Lion Dogs

I believe we have entered the "Moon of the Winter Doldrums" marked by short cold days that seem long in passing, and each day is a steel gray carbon copy of the one before. I get up, check the temperature, eat breakfast, and go about a routine of making and providing a living. A sandwich at noon, then I fumble around till supper with the day ending without much accomplished. It's easy to spend time reading or staring out the window just watching winter pass. Night comes early. It's time again to check the temperature and go to bed. Farmers fill their days by going into town and gathering in smoke filled card rooms to have some fellowship, visiting and listening to friends. One of these days it'll start thawing, the roof will leak on the euchre tables and back to the fields they'll go.

Our family have been carpenters ever since we came here from Ohio in the 1860's. That makes about four generations, and always during this time of year a person in our trade finds there isn't much he can do. So we have grown to expect it and consider having work during this time of year to be a lucky thing like found money. But there was always enough stored away in the cellar to see us through. Dad helped neighbors butcher and brought home some meat and head cheese. A sack of soup beans hung on the porch and vegetable soup was always easy to come up with. Grandpa made a delicious pot, but that's another story sometime.

Dad had sold all the fur by mid January so cash had to be saved and stretched as far as it would go. Mom became an expert at that.

Dad trained coon hounds for hunters and turned out some of the best straight cooners there ever was. One spring a gentlemen in West Virginia, a coal miner, wrote Dad that he was sending a big boned black and tan dog named Lion who was young, strong, and had a good voice. We watched for notice of his arrival. In a week or so word was sent out that a dog was waiting for us at the B and O Depot. Dad and I went to get him and brought him home to Hickory Hollow in the front seat of the '36 Chevy. He was a good looking dog, big footed and strong, just as the man had written. He was friendly, had a smart look about him and became a favorite right away. Lion learned fast and by fall he was doing pretty good with the other dogs.

When the coon season came in, the West Virginia gentleman paid a visit to Illinois and followed the clay road out to our place there on Schaad Creek. He was dressed fine and drove an eight cylinder Pontiac. He sat around the supper table with us and told of his many mining experiences, of going deep underground and then driving five or six miles to work with his big drilling machine. After supper he and Dad went hunting and proved that Lion was, by now, a full grown hound.

They stayed out most of the night with Dad showing what a find job he'd done training the cooner and with the miner being pleased as punch at what a fine dog he owned.

The next evening when my brother and I arrived home from school, the Pontiac with the West Virginia license plates was gone. Dad said that the gentleman had paid him well for training Lion and he asked Dad to keep him through the winter and continue to work with him.

Dad did so, and about every two weeks a letter would arrive postmarked West Virginia, and there would be a five dollar bill in it. Those letters became very important along in January and February when things were getting pretty lean.

One Saturday morning it was cold and the snow was deep. Dad had just come in from feeding the old Jersey cow and was taking off his heavy clothes. Just at that time, he looked out and saw the mailman drive up to the mail box. Dad said, "Roy Lee, run out and get the mail for me, will you Hon?"

I didn't put on a coat or hat but only overshoes and ran out to the mail box. I reached in and grabbed the contents and tore back to the house as hard as I could go. Dad took the mail from me as I came in the door. He went through every piece. He went through it again. He was looking for something. He looked at me rather concerned and asked, "No letters?"

I shook my head no and went back to my playing. Dad read the paper for a little while and then stared out the window toward the road for quite awhile. Then he put on his heavy clothes again and retraced my steps out to the mail box. On his way back, he bent over and picked up a white envelope out of the snow. Dad came in, and I'll never forget the look on his face as he opened the envelope from West Virginia. "You want to be very careful when you get the mail, son," he said.

I knew what he meant. I'm very careful, even yet today.

Angel Maudie

A dulcimer is an old-time musical instrument familiar to those who have lived in the mountains towards the eastern part of the United States. I have made a few, maybe six or eight, and I can pick out a dozen simple tunes. The instrument usually has just three strings. One plays the melody while the others just drone or hum along. I really enjoy dulcimers and believe the simplicity and intimacy of the instrument sounds best in a front room with a few friends gathered around.

A few Christmases back I took one of my instruments to play for the shut-ins at the local shelter care home. It was something I had to do at the time. I wasn't trying to be a goody goody or anything like that. Actually they gave to me more of what I needed than I gave to them. Each of the patients, in his or her own way, enjoyed my little concert.

It was early when I finished there, and I thought I might as well go by an old neighbor's house to see if a visit might cheer her some. Maudie was having a struggle with the illness that keeps taking away and taking away till finally there is that time when one must lay down and let it finish. She had been to the hospital, had all the treatments and chemistry, and fought with a calm courage.

But now, these few days before Christmas, she was home laying in a bed her husband had fixed in the front room so she could at least see her family coming and going and moving about. She passed her time watching the Christmas tree with tinsel and shiny decorations twisting and turning in the light.

Maudie had been raised tough and strong in the Carolina mountains and I thought she would be interested in the dulcimer.

Her husband greeted me at the door and I asked if I might see the missus.

"You bet. Come on in. She'll be glad to see you."

So I walked into the front room beside her bed and saw a much different person than I expected. She was drawn, hollow-eyed, and pale. Her hair was much thinner. I felt I should not have come. But as I reached for her bony hand, she returned a smile, tried to raise her head, and said, "Well looky there what you got under your arm."

Her husband asked, "What is it?"

"Why, it's a dulcimer," she said, and then she asked, "Can you play it?"

I told her that I mostly made them and wasn't much at playing a tune. She moved a feeble hand to the bed rails above her head, and made an effort to pull herself up on the pillow a little higher.

"Come on," she said, "surely you can play something."

So I said, "I'll play you everything I know, and it won't take ten minutes." She grinned as she watched my nubby fingers pick out "Skip to My Lou," "Boil That Cabbage Down," and "You Are My Sunshine."

She motioned for her husband and then said to him, "Push this pillow more under my shoulders. I want to have a better look at this thing." I held out the instrument toward her. She rubbed it, then plucked a string. I was surprised to see her gaining interest.

I said, "Now I can't play any Christmas songs. But I can play this much of 'Silent Night,'" as I strummed out the first few notes and stopped.

She raised her head and said, "Alright now young man, move your finger up another fret."

"Like this?" I questioned.

"No," she scolded. "The other way." She had an edge in her voice and it was stronger. I did what she told me. "Now start again at the beginning and do as I say." She drew a few measured breaths. I plucked out "Silent Night, Holy Night, all is calm, all is...." "Now go back to a G," she said.

I did, and for the next three quarters of an hour, with an occasional rest, she tutored and scolded till I got it right. I thought what a magnificent teacher I had, so positive, so alive in what she knew about music. What a privilege it was for me. When I finally played it through from beginning to end, she smiled and relaxed more into her pillow. She was exhausted but very pleased with what she had accomplished.

There was nothing I could say. It was one of those times when words would have been so inadequate. So I sat there with my dulcimer across my lap, half smiling as moisture filled my eyes.

Now her voice was weak again and she said to her husband, "Go get me my hymn book, my old red one." And he did. She took it and with tiredness thumbed through it till she found the Christmas music. With unsure fingers, she took a lead pencil and marked a letter by each musical note of "Silent Night, Holy Night" from beginning to end. It took her awhile and when she finished, she tore out the page and handed it to me. "Now you take this with you. Practice it. Come by next year and play it good for me."

I took it, of course, most treasured gift, and held her hand before going out into that silent and holy December night.

I still have that sheet from her hymn book, the old red one, and I keep it among my most treasured writings. I noticed it again just the other day and thought of the courage it took Angel Maudie to write the notes as a prelude to her own Silent Night, Holy Night.

The Heart Remembers

I am in the third age of my life some years past sixty now. In those longer nights of December, near the winter solstice, I find myself thinking of those who made a difference in my life, who imprinted enough on the positive side of my nature that remembering them brings a pleasant joy. I could not count more than a dozen I suppose, in the fond remembering, but each year near the Christmas season I gift myself in their memories.

For several years in the second age, the middle years of my life, I lived alone in a quiet empty house, some days hearing only my own sounds, and going for long periods without touching another person.

I longed for cordial company and social human contact. I began to focus on what was going on around me and found square dances in the neighborhood. All through my life I enjoyed the simple dances with the pure undiluted music of the violin, the guitar, and the always happy sound of the banjo. The quick measured steps of the dancing matched the muscle, strength, and tempo of the working people I grew up around.

I began dancing the schottische, the reels, the rounds, and waltzes. Unsure at first but gaining confidence, I soon enjoyed again the social pleasures of being with familiar people doing something together in familiar places. We touched hand over hand, an arm around a waist, a hand on my shoulder. We danced the evening away, healing ourselves with every circle of the set.

There is grace in movement and grace in dance. Even the simple steps feed the soul. Something in us reads the movements of others, the geometry of their walk, the swing of the arm, their balance and poise. We learn a lesson in motivation that some can move with us so much in tune no effort is expended. It is like on like, with each drawing energy from the other till something more than two are dancing, and it is a wonderful experience.

On a December evening, I drove east over a prairie winter landscape of crystalline frost reflecting from roadside weeds and branches. The moon would rise later, so it was in the deep winter darkness that I moved, and I was melancholy, wanting to be in the company of others.

She came early to the dance. Only a few of us were there, warming ourselves around the stove and waiting for the fire to chase the chill from the old school house. She came with a group, some being musicians, others with food baskets to set a Christmas table with sandwiches, cookies, desserts, and warm drinks. She moved about, placing this, arranging that. She was efficient in her movements, accurate and graceful, never heard a footstep, never heard a heel touch the wooden floor.

Friends called her Lea. I danced with her that evening for only a little while and found her movements anticipated mine. We danced and turned and found in the swinging that perfect balance without effort.

The temperature warmed, the floor boards responded and moved with us. We began the hour when the whole of it would be in harmony, when the breathing and movements of three dozen dancers moisten the air and mute the sound, when the stove burns less fierce, when instruments warm and find their voice, when fingers flex and feel the strings just right, when people warm to one another and there is no tension in the room. The rosin is right on the horse hair and pulls long clear notes from the violin to meld with the resonance of the guitar. The music flows sweet and full with an uplifting strength that carried us all just a little above the floor, faces flushed with color and smiles. So much was given one to another with no one left out. So much exchanged and none of it bought nor sold. That is the real gift of Christmas the heart remembers, does not forget, and I was dancing with Lea.

We danced at other times, just occasionally through another fall and winter, and I believed there was a mutual appreciation, though I had never voiced that feeling.

During the summer I heard she was dealing with a condition that had taken two of her sisters and now the malignancy was hers. I worried, felt concern, remembered the trust, the way she moved, and I wanted to go to her to let her know the wonderful experience the dancing had been. But I could not. I was not family.

My many thoughts of her were prayers again and again but she left us anyway, she left us all and I miss her.

This time of year, some twelve, maybe fifteen years past the last we danced, I still notice the dark December sky and see the stars and planets rain down their light. In the mesmerizing stillness, I think of her and feel the gentle hand on my shoulder. I believe she knows my feelings. "Thank you, Lea," I whisper to her, "Merry Christmas."

Fine Folk and Shivarees

She came here from across the river, somewhat a stranger, but had such a goodness about her that she was accepted as a pleasant addition to the community. She found a job in town. It was an ordinary job, but with her easy smile and kind manner, she turned it into a better than average way to make a living. She has worked at it for awhile now. I don't know how long. I suppose if I sat right down and counted, it would be something close to three years. The people she waits on and speaks to with a good morning smile go about their day with spirits raised a little. She's the kind of person who can do that.

This weekend she's getting married and everyone is happy for her. She's marrying a good-natured farm boy, a farm hand with the same kind of ready smile and honest face that she carries. I wish them both the best and have no doubt they'll have it. When I heard the good news about the wedding, I said I thought that they'd be the kind of kids who would enjoy a shivaree. Then somebody asked, "What's a shivaree?" I felt very old. A shivaree is hard to explain, but it was something of a celebration that all newlyweds in the early days of Hickory Precinct expected within a week or so after the wedding day.

It seems as though one of the many Coxes was always getting married down on the bottom, and a shivaree was naturally in order for those good-natured folks. They knew it was something they just had to endure.

HICKORY ROAD

Friends and neighbors waited till later in the evening when it was certain that the couple would already be in bed. With very little advanced planning, the group gathered at a meeting place within a short distance of the young married couple's place of residence. Each family that participated had a special brand of noise they brought to the affair. It was kept in a place ready for use at a moment's notice.

The Houstons brought two or more large disc blades hanging on a buggy axle and hammers to be used to ring them. Someone else brought a wash boiler and another brought tin tubs. They brought sticks of stove wood for beating on their implements. Some carried shotguns, cowbells, pots, pans, kettles or anything else that imagination could dream up to make an ungodly sound. Everyone kept their noisemakers quiet as could be till the right time. They walked closer and closer to the bedroom window of the sleeping couple. When the assembled crowd was close enough, a signal was given. All thunder broke loose with shotguns firing and cowbells ringing. Someone pounded on washtubs, kettles and pans. Others whistled and screamed, and of course, the Houston boys hammered on the terribly loud steel discs. As a bonus, every coon hound within a mile broke into a barking, baying song. It was a commotion that would strike fear or worse into most anyone. In those early days it sometimes took awhile to roust the young couple out, and this evening was no exception.

After a few minutes of the racket, the crowd could see a match being struck inside, and then the glow of a kerosene lamp filled the room. If the newlyweds were good-natured about it—and they usually were—they would invite their friends and neighbors in. This evening, the newly married husband leaned out the window smiling and said, "You all come on in now," whereupon he met us at the door with one suspender of his overall snapped over a shoulder, and the new bride behind him looking perplexed in a new flannel nightgown. They offered cigars to the men folk and some candy or apples to the rest of the crowd. Somebody had brought along enough treats to make plenty. It was a social time, a time of story telling, bragging, and the like. The women folk offered much advice to the blushing bride, and of course, the men of much experience gave pointers to the boy.

Those shivarees were something to observe, especially for a wide-eyed kid. And the best ones were for the common folks. I don't remember going to any fancy places.

Nobody has them anymore. It's too bad they were put aside.

Winter Comforts

It is near midnight in late December. I have just returned home from a country schoolhouse. It is a very old building with uneven floors and drafty windows. The doors do not close as tightly as they did fifty years ago when a teacher and children spent time in the building. It is hard to heat, but there is a country warmth about it that causes people to return. It sits back off the road. No other houses are near so there is silence and clearness to the air that makes one breathe it deeply. The stars are resplendent tonight, and their light on the old snow colors it a soft winter gray.

Now in its second life, the building serves as a community center and a place for old friends of rural persuasion to meet and dance every week or so. Tonight was our Christmas dance, so named because it's just a few days before the holiday. It was marked by a potluck dinner to enjoy, and the feeling of joy and comfort is still with me at this late hour. I was drawn to that place by the honesty of the music and the decency of the people, by a little nostalgia, and a small measure of melancholy.

Tonight as I came home over frozen country roads, I thought of how our lives intertwine with old friends and new friends, the coming and going, how we square-danced, hand over hand, a hand on a shoulder or an arm around a waist. In our closeness we all found a certain fellowship and comfort – comfort akin to that of old familiar quilts.

One time years ago, a scholar asked me, "Why do people move?"

"What do you mean," I asked, "from house to house, from job to job?"

She repeated, "What makes you move?" and left me to ponder the question. It frustrated me. But now twenty years later, I have distilled the thought a thousand times. One word that most often comes to mind is emotion. Emotion makes us move. The emotion of melancholy moves me to find a comfort in others, to reach for a hand to dance with. Joy moves us toward another. To appliqué a hand on hand, then turn about and stitch together a friendship. There is an emotion in the Christmas season that moves us all in the expression of peace and goodwill.

My aunt quilted. She was moved to quilt by the war. While her beloved husband was halfway round the world, far from the house by the creek, she was moved by the emotion of loneliness. In the evening, after feeding the lambs, she cut and pieced and made patterns by the light of a kerosene lamp. She put those patterns together – block by block with the corners always touching. She moved the needle nine stitches to the inch, quilting, quilting till emotion was satisfied and she slept.

Square dancing and old quilts have a lot in common. I imagine if one could see the dancers from above, there would be a pattern in the tracings of the feet as they step and turn, again and again; a kaleidoscope of patterns of the floor boards. Hand over hand in a grand right and left, the Texas star, eight hands round, four couples spinning, a symmetry of repeated forms set to lively music. The color of shirts and skirts and boots and shoes within the borders of the room make the patterns form and reform like the patterns of our lives, with the corners always touching. I realized again that square dances and old quilts are closely related.

HICKORY ROAD

I am home now. Before going in, I stand here in the winter night at the end of a very good evening with a feeling that all my good gifts are in place. I have square danced the evening away, and my aunt's old quilt is waiting on the bed. These are my winter comforts, and I move from one to the other.

Square dancing and old quilts have a lot in common.

Ice Storms and Kids

We had our first ice storm of the season recently in the form of sleet and freezing rain. It wasn't long in coming, but it sure was slow at melting off. Some folks had fallen and broken bones. Others had just ended up with sore muscles and aching joints from falls or near falls. I walked on the ice so much with a cautious stiffness that a hip-joint became tender, but luckily, I never did fall all the way down. A few times I slipped and did some pretty fancy footwork and arm waving in an effort to keep upright. We had a more severe ice storm back about 1949. I started out from home near seven o'clock in the morning on the three mile walk to meet the school bus at Bierhaus Corner. When I turned from the bottom road and started for Houck Hill, the road had such a crown in it that I found it easiest just to walk in the ditches. I reached the big hill and got up it about a quarter of the way before I lost my footing and came bumping back down the hill, sliding on all fours. Undaunted, I tried again. This time I went over to the woven wire fence and used it to hold on as I moved, hand-over-hand, till I reached the top. When I finally did get to Bierhaus Corner about an hour late, a friend there told me that the bus wasn't going to run that day. It was another seven miles to town and school, so I thought I might as well go on back home.

Dad used to tell of a time when he and his siblings were younger that it had come just such an ice storm. First came a light snow and then some rain and mist to put a covering of ice on all the hill country. Black Oak trees, rocks, and rail fences looked like slick and shiny patent leather, making a landscape beautiful, yet so treacherous. Dad, along with his brothers, Elmo and Dick, and sister Gladys, all started out of the house for Hickory School. Each of them carried a little round lunch pail made of tin, as was customary in those days. Mother Dena had put a couple of fried egg and biscuit sandwiches, a sugar cookie, and an apple in each little pail and pressed the lids on carefully. "Now you children," she said, "don't go down the ridge as you usually do. It's too icy this morning. Go over and go down the draw like Pop does with the horses and rig. It'll be longer, I know, but you'll not be so apt to break your necks. Now do as I say and get going or you'll be late."

With that, the kids went out the door, but you know how kids are. They got out of sight of the house and were having such a good time slipping and sliding around on the ice that they thought it would be a lot more fun to go down the ridge. When they got to where the hill crested, they used caution and approached it slowly, taking short little steps, all the while grinning with the fun and excitement of the moment.

Then, almost as if by arrangement, all their feet slipped out from under them at about the same time with lunch pails and arms flying around. Bing! Bang! The lids came off the pails and out rolled the biscuits, fried eggs, cookies and apples. The kids tried to regain their footing and lunches, but it was futile. They hung onto brush and weeds for safety and watched their noon meals gain speed going down the long Taylor Hill. More than two dozen pieces were in the race. The apples took an early lead with sugar cookies rolling close behind. The three sections of the round biscuit sandwiches stuck together for awhile but as they gained speed, they slowly separated. The crusty, brown tops and bottoms veered off a little to the left and right, leaving the fried egg centers rolling a hard true course down the steep hill. By then, it was as if there was a spirit to the race. The apples, the cookies, the liberated chariot wheel-like biscuits racing to the scene of battle, bounced higher and higher at each cow trail, like wild dancing yo yo's, crossing and re-crossing one another. Now they had reached the apex of their speed and leveled off on the pasture land below. It was the home stretch. The apples were winning in the heated race for the brush and tangle of Indian Run Creek. Sugar cookies came in second. The fried egg centers were having the most fun, but Mother Dena's light, airy biscuits were breaking up in flight and failed to complete the race. It had been a sight to see. Those kids always found something funny in any situation and laughed and cheered as they hung onto the hillside by whatever means they could, as they watched the last morsel of dinner roll to a stop and fall on its side in complete exhaustion, the course completed, the race ended.

The boys and Gladys inched their way on down the hillside and upon reaching the bottom began to reassemble what they could of the four scattered lunches. The day had had a great beginning.

For as Long as We Can

It is dark now, an early darkness that will soon give us the longest night. A thin moon hangs high in the December sky, looking down cold the color of ice. The first wind of winter out of the north gives voice to the oak and elm. I hear their conversations and it keeps me company.

By lamp light I write in the shadows with a yellow pencil. In my quiet comfort, I like the sound it makes moving over the paper, shaping the letters, whispering to me as mental pictures are formed into words and paragraphs of thoughts and feelings.

Somewhere lying in us when we are born is a need for music. At some point we hear it. It calls to us and it is our sound. We are awakened to its strengths and comforts. We wish for the sound again and again and go to where it is.

A sweetly tuned fiddle could raise Grandmother Dena from her sick bed and carry her some distance away to Trotter's Hall where she found the sound and the strength to dance, if only for a little while.

I know the feeling. I have just returned from a Christmas dance, a square dance, the last of the season. I carry with me the music, the tunes, the emotions, the familiar faces, and the good feelings I find there. It is all on deposit and I will recall it in days to come.

We of a certain age are drawn by the music of a few instruments politely played, by a soft voice singing, and a fellowship going back for most of our lives.

We were dressed for the season. The music was right. The dancing was spirited, making for laughter and jolly responses. The maple floor was alive and responded to the dancers with flex and sound. We found the rhythms of a good thing happening.

While I rested between squares, I listened and watched the gracefulness and good nature of the others. I am acquainted with the people, if not by name then by association over the years. I know for some there is a great courage and heart in their coming. They are carrying as much as they can, confident they are not letting it show. Walter is favoring his new hip. Emma is facing the season alone for the first time. Norma has a soldier husband far away. Lucy awaits test results. There is Ben, willing to try again after a long, lonely time, now dancing with a younger woman a bit less than eighty. We breathe a silent cheer for all of them and feel a wetness blur our vision.

There will always be concerns and remembrances at Christmas time, but we will come anyway and dance for as long as we can...for as long as we can.

There is no greater gift we can give one another than being there, letting our hearts reach out to spread a little joy during the Christmas season. May God bless us every one.

The Chandler Place

It was in the fall of the year and the leaves had mostly fallen. I had been painting the outside of the two-story Chandler Place for most of a month. It was being readied for a son and daughter-in-law to move into in the spring. Currently, nobody lived there. I had lost my help to the harvest season, and now I was working alone to finish up the outside. It was nearly done.

The big front yard was temporarily fenced. A good neighbor, Mr. Davies, would bring about a half dozen of his sheep over every morning. They would munch on the long lush grass all the day long. They were good company and so quiet I could hear their breathing, could hear them pull the tufts of grass with every bite.

The sheep were tame by now, often being under my ladder while I painted above them. It seemed they liked a little company as much as I liked having them around.

It was getting cold early of a morn. On bad days, I would work on the upstairs rooms, getting them ready to paint by prepping the walls and woodwork. This home, like many century old homes, had high ceilings with a large crown molding running all around the room. A picture mold was just below it. It had big windows to the north and west.

It was good to look out the windows without curtains to see the sheep in the yard, the village down below, to see the harvested fields, and the Sangamon River gently flowing by.

I could see out the west window looking down on Jim Hobson's wood piles all stacked in neat rows some twenty yards away. Jim was in his late seventies, too old to be splitting and stacking wood. He hadn't known anything but hard work all of his life, and now in his later years he couldn't get out of the habit. He worked slower, took his time, and rested more often since he had a scare with his heart a few years back. But he enjoyed splitting wood.

If you've ever split wood with an axe, you probably know it's a good feeling when the wood is seasoned and dry. It splits well with a wedge at first till you split the round into four or five pieces. You make a dozen or so of those into stove wood lengths. Then you take your axe and with one well placed blow with the muscle in your arm and shoulder just right, the wood splits. The sound is good to hear as you strike it. It's good to hear it as it falls to the ground. You make an armload and take it to the woodpile. It is a resting motion that does the back and arm some good.

Jim Hobson split and stacked oak and hickory. He liked hickory best, although it was harder to come by. It had a straighter grain to it than oak which was sometimes gnarly.

Hickory sounded better when the axe split it. It sounded better when it hit the frozen ground. It sounded better when stacked in the woodpile against the others.

He chose to burn hickory in his own wood stove, especially at night when he could see the fire burning through the isinglass in the stove door. Hickory burns bright. Lincoln read by the light of a hickory fire in the fireplace. Old Jim liked to see bright flames through the stove door. He said it was restful, sort of mesmerizing after a day in the cold.

I spread the drop cloths and painted the ceiling first. I had a good brush. It was almost new and had long soft bristles. It was a joy to use and the paint spread well. I had a good wooden stepladder that put me at just the right height.

After a pleasant afternoon painting the large ceiling, it was now time to quit, clean up the brushes and put the paint away for the night. The sun was going down. The short day was almost done.

I returned the next morning to begin where I left off the day before. The sheep came up to the fence to greet me. I started to go in to begin my work but looked at the sheep standing there expecting me to say something to them. So I did. I rubbed their wooly heads, watched their breath, smelled the rich lanolin. They were satisfied and went back to munching the lush grass in the yard.

The sun had been out, but now it was clouding up in the west and getting colder. A light north wind was blowing and spitting snow now and then.

I went in and climbed the stairs to where I had painted yesterday. I would paint the east wall and the north wall this morning. I got out my brushes, bucket, and ladder and began painting.

It was quiet as it always is when you work alone. I like it that way. It gives me plenty of time for my thoughts, and nothing to disturb my thinking.

It was late when Jim came out to cut his wood. I could see him out the west window. He was dressed in his overall jacket, probably with a sweater underneath, and well worn sharkskin pants. He had on his four buckle overshoes so his feet would stay warm. Yellow shucking gloves with the extra thumb covered his hands, something he was in the habit of wearing from his corn shucking days. On his head he wore a dark cap with ear flaps pulled down and strings flopping from the ends.

He was set to spend the morning splitting and stacking firewood in neat rows, making a cord as he went along.

My arm was getting tired after applying a lot of paint in the morning hours, but it was about noon and time for dinner. When I glanced out the big west window I noticed it was snowing a little harder, and the flakes were bigger, too. Jim had gone in for his dinner. He was nowhere to be seen.

In silence I ate my sandwiches, the peaches, two cookies and a thermos of tea. Then I must have taken a short nap. When I awoke, I looked for Jim. He was already out there dressed warm and cutting his wood. In the falling snow I could still make out the figure of a man raising his axe to split the wood. The falling snow added a new dimension to the winter landscape. I loved to play in new fallen snow when I was a kid. I felt as though Jim was experiencing the same kind of carefree joy as he cut wood in the snow.

I would paint the west wall this afternoon, the one with the big window. I got my bucket, brushes, and my ladder and began to paint in the corner. It was a monotonous job but had to be done. I painted toward the window.

I must have painted a couple of hours to get to the big west window. I looked out through the falling snow to Jim's woodpile. The snow made it hard to see, but I was sure there was a vehicle with flashing red lights in the yard. What could it be? Could it be an ambulance? People were moving about. I watched the unfolding drama for a half hour or so. Finally someone opened the vehicle's back doors. Was it paramedics who slid the gurney in before taking off in a hurry? I wondered what had taken place.

I went back to my painting and finished the west wall to the far corner before quitting time, but I worried about Jim.

HICKORY ROAD

I put my bucket and brush away, then went downstairs and outside. The sheep were waiting with snow piled high on their backs. I looked over toward Jim's house for a long time. It was dark. Nothing moved. No smoke came from the chimney. Snow was on the wood piles – snow on the ground.

When I came to work the next morning, before going up the hill to the Chandler Place I stopped in at Wiseman's Café downtown. I went in and asked the locals if they knew anything about what went on up at old Jim's yesterday. "Wasn't that an ambulance in the yard?" I asked.

They said, "Haven't you heard? Jim died yesterday. He was sitting on the ground leaning against a woodpile. Looked kinda comfortable, but he was dead. Neighbors found him there covered with snow. He died doing what he liked to do. You can't ask for more than that, now can you?" they said. "No sir, you can't ask for more than that."

Jim had split his last stick of fire wood. He was all done. It would be different working at the Chandler Place. It would be just me and the sheep.

Sheep at the Chandler Place

New Salem Christmas

I read in the newspapers recently where the "Christmas at New Salem" weekend will be done away with. It seems that research has proven that the inhabitants of that short lived village where Lincoln grew to manhood were not of the beliefs that would cause them to consider Christmas as any kind of holiday. So in keeping with the pure authenticity of the village, Christmas cannot be a part of any special event. Not true.

I was born near where Lincoln walked and later grew up by the Lincoln Highway, hunted squirrels where he debated free silver with Stephen A. Douglas a quarter mile from our house. I made my first trip to New Salem riding in the back seat of an Essex automobile packed tightly among other kids from Hickory School.

I was raised in a hollow near that school and as the Christmas season nears, I think and remember those first Christmases there in that house in the hollow by Schaad Creek, protected and fed by the earth, the wooded hills, and a family that included Mom and Dad, sisters and brothers, and Grandpa. In later life I would realize that we were very poor during those times, but I never remember ever feeling that way during my early years growing up in that place. The gifts we received were simple and oft times things we needed. The real joy of remembered was the spirit of things at school and church. I am drawn to that hollow as this season nears. I go there, smell the earthen dampness, sit on the hillside, then cut a few boughs of evergreen—the prickly limbs of the aromatic Red Cedar trees—and bring them to where I live now. The fragrance is an instant reminder of the Cedar trees Dad would find along his trap line and bring in for us to have in the front room. The essence of red cedar is Christmas to me and kindles memories of early Christmases in that hollow.

I have attended many of the New Salem Christmases and always came away feeling that it must have been a special place in Lincoln's memory just as that place in the hollow is for me.

I have an old suit of clothes authentic to the 1850's. It is of black woolen material and includes trousers with buttons for suspenders, a vest, and a great coat with pockets in the tails. It is of a generous cut, cut that way for riding horseback. A black hat makes the outfit complete. It is a very warm suit of clothes, and I always wore this to the New Salem Christmas. I was not the only one. My friend, Dr. Glen, a pill roller, wore a similar outfit. And a tall man, complete with a mole on his cheek, would arrive looking very much like a returning Lincoln, except for his wing tip shoes.

A few years back, I went to a New Salem Christmas on a Sunday morning after a light snow had fallen. I was feeling melancholy and not wanting to spend the Sunday alone. I put on my old time suit and drove over. I did not drive up the hill, knowing the upper lot would be full. Instead, I parked below by the bridge where the Cedar trees grow.

The day had not warmed much. The sky was winter gray. I put on a scarf and buttoned up my vest and heavy coat, then put on my top hat. In the blue winter mist beside the stream I looked around me. I noticed the soft clean snow, the kind that hushes everything and makes all motion silent, I noticed the contrast of soft shadows and trees, and the scent of cedar. In the parking lot, there was the bronze statue of Lincoln reading a book and sitting astride a horse. Snow lay on his shoulders, on his head, and on his open book, but still it felt that this was his place.

I turned from the scene and made my way up the draw towards the south border of the village. Snow dusted down on me as I walked through hazel brush and sumac. I saw footprints in the snow and looked around to try to see who was making them. I could barely make out through the thicket a figure dressed in black, a figure much like me, only taller. I thought it might be Dr. Glen or maybe the Lincoln look-alike. I stopped for a closer look at the tracks in the snow. They were boot prints, heavy of heel and wide at the foot, with the toe turned up sharply. It was an unusual print. When I looked up, no figure was visible. I went on up the hill a few steps and soon heard the music coming from Rutledge Tavern and the thumping sound of a jig being danced on the puncheon floor. The smell of wood smoke caught my senses. We burned wood in our trusty Heatrola there in Hickory Hollow. Melancholy was with me again, but sat comfortably and kept its distance. I leaned on the rail fence and looked across to the next ridge where young Ann Rutledge was laid to rest the first time. Lincoln loved Ann and lost her, so he knew sadness here.

I walked around the lot fence to see a cheery crowd enjoying the snow and each other. Women were dressed in old-time frocks and warm woolen shawls. Children were in homespun with cheeks so pink from the chilly air.

I saw friends of mine and together we entered the cozy room and moved near the fireplace. The cabin kept filling with others as music and warmth and Christmas singing invited them in till my friends and I were packed close together. I felt the warmth of those around us and thought to myself that this is what it's like to feel good and whole, and I wished it could go on forever.

But nothing is forever. The fiddle stopped and the singers left. The mood changed and I walked on toward the Onstot cabin where I met Dr. Glen rolling his pills. We exchanged pleasantries, and then I asked if he'd walked up the hillside a little earlier. He gave me a puzzled look, then said he'd gotten there early and parked in the upper lot. I asked how many Lincolns he'd seen there that day.

"Gee, I don't know," he answered. "There's that tall one that always comes. Then there's you, but you're too short to be a Lincoln. Then there's another one around that looks more like Lincoln than any of them. Never got a chance to get close to him but he looks right." So I left him and went about my way.

As I neared the cabin of Samuel Hill and heard the muted sounds of a dulcimer, I saw one Lincoln up ahead in the crowd. This was surely the one in wingtip shoes. But another stood off alone. Tall, dressed in black, a face without expression. I walked toward him, but he was lost around the corner of an outbuilding before I could get close.

When I came to where he had been standing, I saw only boot prints in the snow, the same heavy heeled prints I had seen earlier on the hillside. Here was a shy Lincoln who wasn't very social on this day, yet he seemed so much to belong here.

Darkness was coming early to this wooded village just as it did to our house there in the hollow. By four o'clock it was time to light the lamps and build up the fires. Now I could see the candle lanterns in the cabin windows and the warm golden glow of the fires filling the rooms. The crowd was thinning as I made my way back to the other end of the village where I had entered. There, ahead of me, at the very limit of my vision, in the haze lying over the snow, I could make out the dark figure of a Lincoln moving ahead of me. He was too tall to be Doctor Glen. But who could it be? I did not try to get closer, but just followed along. He entered the thicket of hazel brush and I lost all sight of him. I listened for him moving through the brush and heard nothing except my own breathing. I followed his path. As I entered the brush, a cedar bough brushed my face. I continued on down to the clearing where I had parked. No one was now visible. I was alone again.

Lincoln may not have celebrated Christmas at New Salem during his six years there. Maybe the families of Peter Lukins, Josh Miller, Bob Johnson or Martin Waddell did not celebrate Christmas while at New Salem. But many of those families lived on into later years and enjoyed Christmas as it became a more universal and popular holiday, a time of family and friends and the recalling of old times past, times important in shaping their lives. Lincoln would recall his New Salem days, the warmth and friendships there as a young man, memories and feelings he carried with him to the prairies riding circuit, and on to Springfield where he raised a family and on to the Presidency in Washington.

I recall our family there in Hickory Hollow. We are all gone from there now, for over sixty years. But I go back for a short nostalgic and melancholy visit every now and then, just as I believe Lincoln returns to New Salem. I do not doubt his presence there—especially at Christmas time.

Gwyn's Skating

A few Sundays ago, I spent some time with young Gwyn on the frozen backwaters of Hinkson Creek. Gwyn is a thirteen year old friend of mine that I visit occasionally.

The weather had warmed so the ice was soft, rough and unpredictable. If we stopped for awhile, water seeped through and formed a puddle where we stood. We moved on, me plodding along in overshoes, and she skating beside me.

No matter where I walk, summer or winter, I carry a well worn walking stick. It furnishes a bit of security for me, especially when I walk on strange ice, unfamiliar ice. I didn't know how deep the water was so I tested with each strike of the stick to get a reading, a feedback as to the hardness of the ice, a sound to my instincts to whether it's safe or not, whether it's deep or shallow. I've watched my father do the same.

Moving upstream to where the channel narrowed and the ice turned white, we searched for hard ice. Surely the water was not deep and the bank was nearby.

"This is neat," Gwyn said, "Just like the Dutch canals I've read about where people can skate for miles to visit or shop or just for fun."

She raced on ahead of me, her red jacket the only bright color in the winter landscape, farther away, smaller and smaller, till she rounded a curve and was out of my sight. She soon reappeared as she came back toward me, leaning forward, side to side, with long flashing strokes. She turned and stopped beside me in a spray of ice chips.

The creek became narrower yet. The ice was very rough. Sticks and leaves had melted down into it, leaving a cookie cutter pattern of their own intricate shapes. Then we both walked for a few yards to explore a beaver dam and to see where the animals had gnawed on Cottonwood trees nearby. We stood and enjoyed the sun before walking back toward bigger water and greater ice.

Near the south bank of a wide expanse, where the winter sun never shines, we found our ice, green and hard as flint, almost black with clarity. We looked into it as a precious gem of diamond or jade, on through it to movements and wiggly things below. We were so enthralled by it that we forgot about skating for the moment. The ice would never be the same another time, or even again. It was only for that hour on a Sunday afternoon.

Then Gwyn began to skate, slowly at first and in silence on the perfect ice. Steel runners made perfect sounds in graceful turns and wide arcs as a young flexible body, strong and fresh with misty breath and winter reddened cheeks, went faster and faster, stretching and reaching on past the edges of her adolescence. She would never be the same another time or ever again. But only for that hour on a Sunday afternoon.

The sun was low by then, somewhere far behind the hill. We started back to where we had come onto the ice. We hadn't talked much, Gwyn and I, but conversations are not always necessary. Sometimes words and talking fall short in expressing what we feel.

Gwyn skating on Hinkson Creek

Gooseberries

Could I bring you a summer evening
with jewels of dew drops
Just beginning to kiss the earth?

Or maybe a thousand fireflies on a string
Or an evening star, set in a grey-blue sky.

How about the moon
rising to the cadence of the whippoorwill?
All for you—would you like that too?

Well, instead of those things above,
just take these gooseberries now, my love.
RLF, 1973

    I have some friends that are, of all things, especially fond of gooseberries, those "puckery" little pearl green marbles that grow on "stickery" wild bushes for the most part. There is the tame variety, too, but I still like to go for them out in the pasture and timber.
    Neighbor Salzman had a giant clump of gooseberry bushes growing on a creek bank at the edge of his cow pasture. I've taken a half gallon of the little fruit off it each year for several years now. The creek keeps washing closer and soon the bush

will be gone, but for now, it's doing a good job of holding the earthen bank together. Because the bush and I are on such good terms (I often pass it no matter the season), on occasion I have taken a few cow chips from the pasture and scattered them around the roots. This season being what it is, and with the help of the cow chips, the berries are bigger than I've ever seen them. I picked a little over a quart in no time at all. They remain good when they're kept cool.

A few days later during a rainy spell, I took my berries out of the cellar and headed for an old time country kitchen at Clayville, near Springfield. I sat on the porch there, out of a summer shower and set about stemming the hard little berries. The stemming takes longer than the picking, but at least one can sit down and do it. My friends at the kitchen have never dealt with gooseberries before but knew they made good pies. After finding an 1850 recipe calling for two and a half cups, they set me out to measure and went ahead with heating up the oven and making the pie crust. The old time recipe called for only a bottom crust with the berries poured into it, then baked some more. It turned out to be a fine experience as six of us gathered around the kitchen table and enjoyed wild gooseberry pie. They commented as to how much work it was to pick and stem so many little bitty berries for only one pie. I tried to explain that there is more to it than just eating a piece of pie.

I delivered a quart of stemmed gooseberries to some friends in Virginia one time, and they went on and on about how much trouble I had gone to. "Why, it must have taken hours," they remarked. Yes, it had, but what pleasant hours. To take an hour or so after super and walk along the meadow by the creek, pick a few berries, listen to the water running over rocks, find a dove's nest—well, I have a hard time calling that a lot of trouble. When handing the berries to my friends, I feel that

I've had all the fun, and "Sorry, but all you're getting are these 'puckery' little fruits."

Find a gooseberry bush, put it between you and the sun, especially after a shower, and see the berries hang there gathering light. Hear the whippoorwill begin his evening song—again, again, again.

I wonder if we are calling some things work today that were pleasures not so long ago.

March of March

MAR 2 Today – a celebration of the sun. I have been walking on frozen snow for two months. The frailty of snowflakes built into awesome cliffs and drifts. Now it rots, disintegrates, dissolves and moves to make water, to make streams, to make rivers, to the power of floods and oceans. I especially noticed this morning as I left for work that clumps of grass are beginning to reach above the snow in Clement's pasture, making brown areas in the fields of white. Later in the day I saw ice bound puddles grow, reach out to join other water, then gain speed and sound as they rushed off in the parade for the Gulf.

MAR 5 Started home from work early with the sun coming in through the rear glass and flooding the space around me. What a good feeling to relax and feel the weather and not have to brace against the cold, the dark, the wind. Kids walked in puddles watching their feet move in miracles of unending water. The complete acceptance of this new weather, a swelling, a rising pressure in the temple of living things. It was hard to keep a smile back with each discovery of a new sight released from winter's hold.

MAR 6 The brook beside the house that couldn't make a sound all winter is now talking to me from under the willow roots. A collar of white hangs along each bank and water traces along under those chambers to make a stronger echo. Liquid sounds emerge from choir lofts of ice. But each night the songs are captured, the sounds withheld. Cold and stiffness return.

MAR 8 Tonight it's growing bitter cold again, a reminder that winter is not ready to move away, but sunset was later and sunrise will be earlier. The sun is winning. Tomorrow it will warm easily.

MAR 10 Went to bed with mist changing to light rain. Before I slept, I saw an unnatural flash. An arc was struck and I heard the muted sound of first thunder shouldering its way through fog. Rain increased and made a melody in the eave spout.

MAR 12 Today I opened the doors to other parts of the house and let the heat from the stove into cooler rooms. I can afford to live in the whole house. At least for today. I wanted to open the windows and let all outdoors inside—but not yet. Maybe in a week or so.

MAR 13 Planted tomato seeds in peat pots to begin the growing season. Soon they'll rise and lean toward the window.

MAR 15 Today was such that I was never warm. The chill wind cut through as if I were lightly clothed. Even though the temperature was not freezing, I never really warmed. In the evening by the stove and lamplight, I found the first comfort of the day.

MAR 20 Sometime over the past week someone has been stealing the snow. I had not noticed, but it is mostly all gone. How could those enormous piles and drifts, that awful amount, get away so silently. In return we've been given mud. It's very warm out now. For awhile it is ideal, but I know before the day is over the wind will blow. These days, this month, is as changeable as a girl I once knew.

MAR 25 Before I slept last night, a moth fluttered against my window trying to gain the light of my lamp. The first insect, this butterfly of Chinese paper alive outside my window. An insect as frail as dust and I have survived another winter.

MAR 28 I heard the first frogs by the pond this morning. In awhile geese answered and put their reflections on the water. Yellow daffodils are pushing through the sod. Red tulips are close behind. March of March.

The Silence of the Wood

Remembering Special People, Favorite Places
and the Holiday Times of My Life

Mr. Frasher's mill was across the road from where our first Christmas memories formed. Dad, his brother, and Grandfather Will all worked there. The small house we lived in was built by them with wide oak boards from that sawmill.

Oak trees grew tall and straight in the hollows and on the gentle slopes. A smart horse and a little gravity snaked the logs to the yard where peavey, pike and muscle put them on the saw carriage. Mr. Frasher's Twin City tractor drove the belt that turned the blade, dividing the logs into boards. In the process, the air was filled with sawdust, and the unforgettable scent of fresh sawn oak stays with me yet.

Our family has worked with wood in all the common ways for six generations. We feel it, understand it, and find favor with it. Wood is an old friend that responds to our touch and gives us comfort, identity, and purpose.

As the century ends, the old mill beside Hickory Road is silent and has been for sixty years or more. So too are the men and tools that made it work...all gone away.

Christmas is for remembering so I go there in the short December days to walk and visit in the silence of the wood. There are still things familiar—old trees much larger now, line posts of the south fence, and the murmuring of water in Schaad Creek.

The blue jay calls. Crows visiting among themselves and chickadees precede me, looking back at each perch saying, "dee, dee, dee," as interested in me as I am in them.

We had a kinship with all the wild creatures living there. They helped us identify ourselves, told us where we were, piqued our interest, made tracks in the snow, expanded our minds, and called to us in the night. With a special blessing, they provided food for our table and sustained us.

As I walk, an earthy fragrance rises up on moist air, finger printing the place where I am and opening another room of Christmas memories that make me stand awhile. I am waist-high among Cedar trees, dozens of them propagated by an age-old mother tree on the evening side of the hill.

The house of oak and a thousand feelings has fallen in. Mother's sink is in the rubble. I remember her happiness in getting it, a minor thing, a major event wrapped in a never fading memory of a simple joy.

The youngest son was born in the front bedroom. As Mother recovered from the birthing, she opened her eyes to see faces of family, a healthy baby boy and a room filled with the peach and amber glow of kerosene lamps. She said that it was like a dream and that she felt whole and wonderful again. I remember her joy in telling me of the experience, and somewhere in the dust and decay that gift of happiness remains.

The low winter sun falls west, angles down the hollow, and touches the naked winter branches of the tree line in Uncle Troy's pasture. Warmth and light diminish. Darkness begins in the dome of the sky and the first stars appear, faint - twinkling - shimmering. As darkness closes, they shine brighter and multiply to an endless river of stars.

In the eastern sky high above Warner's Hill, I find the Christmas star shining brighter than all the rest. It is immensely beautiful. It is immensely quiet and all is calm. By starlight I walk my way out of the Cedars, out of the hollow, and the silence of the wood.

A saw mill is nearby and neighbors as interesting as those his father knew.

About The Author

Roy L. French was born in his grandmother's front bedroom in a home on the west end of Virginia, a small central Illinois town. It was in the spring of 1933, the worst year of the Great Depression. A few days later his father and mother, Dave and Marie, bundled him up and took him home to a place out on Hickory Road. The years passed and he, along with his brothers and sisters, went about gathering life's experiences. Grandpa lived with them, adding another dimension to their lives.

Roy's father, Dave, and his grandfather, Will, worked at Clem Frasher's Saw Mill, did carpenter work, and some farm work during those hard times. But what Dave enjoyed most and did best was hunting and trapping in the winter months. He had a love and understanding of the outdoors and passed this on to his children. Dave was also a master story teller and told and retold of his outdoor experiences. Roy heard them over and over, and in later years wrote down some of the stories. Eventually, he wrote a weekly newspaper article called "Trapper Dave's Journal" that was widely read and appreciated. In September of 1976 his dad died, but not before telling Roy that he had a gift for writing and not to let it go to waste. After a time, Roy began penciling out "The Hickory Journal" on the kitchen table. It contained reflections on rural life in Cass County during an earlier, simpler time.

Roy, now 77 years old, was a carpenter by trade like four generations before him. He is now retired and lives in Virginia with his wife, Barbara, a few blocks from where he was born. It is not far from Hickory Road, the Hollow, and Schaad Creek. When he walks its banks and wanders the adjoining hills and fields, he finds there the same strength his father and those before him found. There are also new adventures of day to day life that Roy writes about. A saw mill is nearby and there are neighbors as interesting as those his father knew. As Roy has often written, "Some things change, other things never do."

Although the Hollow is much different now than it was in the thirties, Grandpa's Catalpa tree is still standing sentinel seventy years later to the many memories made there. Roy can go there yet and find them.

The French's place in the Hollow taken about 1980. A fallen-in house and sheds are all that remain. Schaad Creek has washed away the garden patch and is much wider and deeper now.

Dave and Marie holding the twins, Doris Kay and Deloris Fay. Standing in front: Roy Lee, Jackie David, and Billy John. This photo was taken on Grandma's front sidewalk.

Would you like to see your manuscript become a book?

If you are interested in becoming a PublishAmerica author, please submit your manuscript for possible publication to us at:

acquisitions@publishamerica.com

You may also mail in your manuscript to:

**PublishAmerica
PO Box 151
Frederick, MD 21705**

www.publishamerica.com

PublishAmerica